Interacting Selves

The counselling and psychotherapy professions have experienced a rapid growth and expansion throughout Europe and internationally. State regulation of these professional practices has required *personal development hours* for those in training and *continuing professional development* for all qualified practitioners, as well as *supervision* of their practice.

Interacting Selves provides concepts and principles of personal and professional development (PPD) in training and supervision as part of an approach to lifelong learning for all those involved in psychotherapeutic work. Leading European trainers and practitioners draw on their shared background in systemic therapy to articulate a strong theoretical base for PPD. The volume functions not simply as a coherent description of the philosophy and rationale underlying PPD, but also as a practice workbook whose chapters contain an array of elegantly crafted exercises, portable across the broad range of disciplines that give life to the social care and mental health fields at the same time as meeting the PPD needs of counsellors and psychotherapists of different theoretical persuasions.

The approaches work through constant attention to PPD as an interpersonal process where thoughts, ideas and emotions need to be nurtured. PPD can involve working at the extremes, and the book provides a secure basis for confronting abuse and violence head-on. Each chapter shows how personal and professional development promotes a focus on emotional competence, positive emotion, resilience and ethical practice.

Interacting Selves introduces and develops the concepts and principles of PPD in training and supervision as part of an approach to lifelong learning for all psychotherapists undergoing or providing PPD. This pioneering book will appeal to psychotherapy trainees, trainers, practitioners and supervisors in the mental health field and social care professionals.

Arlene Vetere is Professor of Family Therapy and Systemic Practice at Diakonhjemmet University College, Oslo, Norway; Visiting Professor of Clinical Psychology at Universita degli Studi di Bergamo, Italy; and Affiliate Professor of Family Studies at the University of Malta. She is a chartered clinical psychologist and systemic psychotherapist, and systemic supervisor, registered in the UK.

Peter Stratton is Emeritus Professor of Family Therapy at Leeds University and Leeds Family Therapy & Research Centre, a systemic psychotherapist who is qualified in psychodynamic psychotherapy. He is a developmental psychologist with broad research interests and involvement in statutory processes that affect families. He is a chartered psychologist; Fellow of the British Psychological Society; UKCP accredited family therapist; and AFT accredited family therapy supervisor.

'Arlene Vetere and Peter Stratton give us a new, enjoyable and useful perspective on an often overlooked dimension in systemic training and practice. Bringing together different voices and expertise, they offer an account of personal and professional development that is both comprehensive and experiential; each author adds to each chapter practical exercises that transform mere reading into a proper learning and personal experience, thus perfectly reflecting the subject and purpose of the text. An essential reading for any trainer and supervisor, both within and outside the systemic field.'

Paolo Bertrando, Director, Systemic-Dialogical
School of Bergamo, Italy

'The central premise of the book is that continuing professional development is about learning. It presents material and application activities that are suitable for trainees, practitioners, supervisors and consultants in maintaining or advancing their knowledge and skills for their psychotherapy work across a number of contexts. The book focuses on personal application with case examples and exercises that invite readers to reflect upon their own ways of working and to contemplate and enhance what they do. The book succeeds in its purpose. The book is practical, engaging and readable. I recommend it highly!'

D. Russell Crane, PhD, Professor of Family Therapy, School of
Family Life, Brigham Young University, Provo, UT, USA.
Editor *Contemporary Family Therapy: An International Journal*

'Who are you as a professional? Where are you coming from and where do you want to go from here? These are the questions on the horizon of each and every word in this book. Securely rooted in systemic understanding, this book offers a rich variety of ideas on professional and personal development (PPD). This book is a treasure trove for therapists, counsellors, trainers, supervisors and consultants from whatever persuasion.'

Prof. Dr. Peter Rober, Clinical Psychologist and
Family Therapist, KU Leuven, Belgium

Interacting Selves

Systemic solutions for personal
and professional development in
counselling and psychotherapy

Edited by
Arlene Vetere and
Peter Stratton

 Routledge
Taylor & Francis Group

LONDON AND NEW YORK

First published 2016
by Routledge
2 Park Square, Milton Park, Abingdon, Oxon, OX14 4RN

and by Routledge
711 Third Avenue, New York, NY 10017

Routledge is an imprint of the Taylor & Francis Group, an informa business

British Library Cataloguing in Publication Data
A catalogue record for this book is available from the British Library

Library of Congress Cataloging in Publication Data
Interacting selves: systemic solutions for personal and professional
    development in counselling and psychotherapy/edited by Arlene
    Vetere and Peter Stratton. – First Edition.
    pages cm
    1. Self-perception. 2. Self-actualization (Psychology) 3. Psychotherapy.
    I. Vetere, Arlene, editor. II. Stratton, Peter, editor.
    BF697.5.S43158 2016
    158.3071'5–dc23
    2015027351

ISBN: 978-0-415-73084-6 (hbk)
ISBN: 978-0-415-73085-3 (pbk)
ISBN: 978-1-315-68762-9 (ebk)

Typeset in Times New Roman and Gill Sans
by Florence Production Ltd, Stoodleigh, Devon, UK

Contents

Notes on contributors   vii

1   Prologue and introduction to the systemic approach to personal
    and professional development   1
    ARLENE VETERE, PETER STRATTON, HELGA HANKS, PER JENSEN,
    KYRIAKI PROTOPSALTI-POLYCHRONI AND JIM SHEEHAN

2   PPD as processes of learning that enable the practitioner
    to create a self that is equipped for higher levels of
    professional mastery   7
    PETER STRATTON AND HELGA HANKS

3   Mind the map: circular processes between the therapist,
    the client and the therapist's personal life   33
    PER JENSEN

4   Supervision: present within movements   51
    ANNE HEDVIG HELMER VEDELER

5   Working at the extremes: the impact on us of doing the work   65
    HELGA HANKS AND ARLENE VETERE

6   A supervisor's progression: from personal and professional
    development training in group settings to the inclusion of
    the self of the therapist in supervision   85
    BARBARA KOHNSTAMM AND ARLENE VETERE

7   Supervision and attachment narratives: using an attachment
    narrative approach in clinical supervision   99
    ARLENE VETERE AND RUDI DALLOS

8   Self and world: narrating experience in the supervisor/supervisee
    relationship   109
    JIM SHEEHAN

9   Conclusion: consolidation, celebration and momentum   131
    PETER STRATTON, ARLENE VETERE, HELGA HANKS,
    ANNE HEDVIG HELMER VEDELER, PER JENSEN,
    KYRIAKI PROTOPSALTI-POLYCHRONI AND JIM SHEEHAN

    Index   139

Contributors

Arlene Vetere is Professor of Family Therapy and Systemic Practice at Diakonhjemmet University College, Oslo, Norway. In addition, she is Visiting Professor of Clinical Psychology at Universita Degli Studi, Bergamo, Italy, and Affiliate Professor of Family Studies at Malta University, Malta. Arlene is a chartered clinical psychologist registered with the UK Health and Care Professions Council; a systemic psychotherapist registered with the UK Council for Psychotherapy; and a systemic supervisor registered with the UK Association for Family Therapy. She was President of the European Family Therapy Association for two terms, 2004–2010. Arlene has co-directed a family violence intervention service for over 20 years, and has developed 'attachment narrative therapy' in association with Professor Rudi Dallos.

Peter Stratton is Emeritus Professor of Family Therapy at Leeds University and Leeds Family Therapy Research Centre, a systemic psychotherapist who is qualified in psychodynamic psychotherapy. He is a developmental psychologist with broad research interests and involvement in statutory processes that affect families. His main current research is to develop measures of family and relationship functioning for use by therapists (the SCORE project). Peter is Joint Editor of *Human Systems*, Chair of the European Family Therapy Association Research Committee and Managing Director of the Psychology Business Ltd. He is a member of the CAMHS Outcomes and Evaluations, the CYP-IAPT Critical Friends and the Relate Research Advisory Groups, and recently Academic and Research Development Officer for the Association for Family Therapy and Chair of the UK Council for Psychotherapy Research Faculty. BSc, PhD, Dip Psychotherapy, FBPsS; chartered psychologist; fellow of the British Psychological Society; UKCP accredited family therapist; AFT accredited family therapy supervisor.

Rudi Dallos is Professor of Clinical Psychology and Research Director of the Clinical Psychology Doctorate Programme at Plymouth University, UK. He has worked as a family therapist for over 30 years and has developed an integrative approach – attachment narrative therapy – with Arlene Vetere. He has published a range of papers and books, including *Researching Psychotherapy* *and Counselling* (with Arlene Vetere), *An Introduction to Family Therapy* and, most recently, *Attachment and Family Therapy*.

Helga Hanks is a consultant clinical psychologist (chartered), analytic psychotherapist and systemic family therapist in the Department of Community Paediatrics, St James's University Hospital, Leeds. She is registered with the Health and Care Professions Council (HCPC) and a member of the AFT. Until her retirement from her full-time post, she was also a visiting senior lecturer at the Institute of Psychological Sciences, Leeds University. She is one of the founder members of the Leeds Family Therapy Research Centre (LFTRC) at Leeds University, which came into existence in 1979. She has been Clinical Director of the Centre until 2005. She is one of the core staff who developed the MSc in Systemic Family Therapy at the Institute of Psychological Sciences, Leeds University. Since 1980, she has provided systemic training for a wide variety of professionals across the world. The *Journal of Human Systems* was first published in 1990, and she was a founder member of that journal. She continues to be on the editorial board. She has published and researched widely both in the areas of family therapy and child abuse.

Per Jensen is Professor at the Master Programme in Family Therapy and Systemic Practice, Diakonhjemmet University College, Oslo, Norway. He has a doctorate in Systemic Psychotherapy from the Tavistock Centre, London and the University of East London, UK. He has written several articles and books on the practice of family therapy.

Barbara Kohnstamm is a registered family, couples and individual therapist, and a registered supervisor with the Dutch Family Therapy Association (NVRG) and the Family Therapy Association of Ireland (FTAI). She is a registered EFT therapist (ICEEFT), supervisor and trainer. She also trained in cognitive analytic therapy in the UK (ACAT). She was Chairperson of the Family Therapy Association of Ireland and Chair of the Chamber of National Family Therapy Associations, within the European Family Therapy Association. She received an award for her special contributions to this organisation in 2007. After living and working in Ireland for many years, she is now living in The Netherlands and has a private therapy and supervision practice.

Kyriaki Protopsalti-Polychroni is a psychologist, couple and family psychotherapist, trainer and supervisor. Ms Protopsalti-Polychroni is a senior member of the Scientific Team of the Athenian Institute of Anthropos in Greece, the first center to practise family therapy in Europe. She is a founding member of the European Family Therapy Association (EFTA) and the Association's Immediate Past President. She is also currently the Vice Chair of the Chamber of Training Institutes (EFTA-TIC). She is a member of the American Academy of Family Therapists (AFTA); former vice president of the national branch of the European Association of Psychotherapists (EAP); founding member of the American National Registry of Certified Group Psychotherapists (CGP); a long-standing clinical member of the American Group Psychotherapy Association (AGPA); founding member of the Hellenic Association of Systemic Therapy; and former member of the Executive Council of the Association of Greek Psychologists. Since 2008, Ms Protopsalti-Polychroni is Joint Editor of *Human Systems: The European Journal of Therapy, Consultation and Training*, which was recently adopted as the official journal of the EFTA. She trains and supervises professionals in systemic group, couple and family therapy.

Jim Sheehan is a social worker, family therapist and systemic psychotherapy supervisor. He has been Director of Family Therapy Training at the Mater Hospital and University College Dublin from 1987 to 2012 and part-time Professor of Family Therapy and Systemic Practice at the Diakonhjemmet University College, Oslo, from 2005 to the present time. Since 2012, he has been Adjunct Senior Lecturer in the Faculty of Medicine, University College Dublin. In his Dublin-based private practice, he works with families, couples and children, as well as supervising counsellors and psychotherapists.

Anne Hedvig Helmer Vedeler is an Assistant Professor at Diakonhjemmet University College in Oslo, Norway, where she is the Director of its Personal and Professional Development Program. She also runs a family- and network-oriented program in collaboration with Nesna University College and Rana Municipality. She has her own private practice called Dialogical Practice, offering therapy, consultation, coaching, supervision and teaching.

Chapter 1

Prologue and introduction to the systemic approach to personal and professional development

Arlene Vetere, Peter Stratton, Helga Hanks,
Per Jensen, Kyriaki Protopsalti-Polychroni and
Jim Sheehan

Why you should use this book

Welcome to our book, which has been a process in which each of us has extended our ideas through our interactions around its content. Our aspiration is that the book will add new dimensions to helping those engaging with personal and professional development (PPD) to create a substantial upgrading of practice at all levels. Although PPD takes different forms in different therapies and contexts of practice, we have tried to engage with this diversity by creating comparable diversity in what we offer. Our intention is that the book will provide practicable help whether you are a trainee wanting to make best use of the PPD content of your course, a therapist deriving maximum benefit from supervision and continuing professional development (CPD) events or a trainer/supervisor wanting to be able to offer the most effective provision.

Although between us we have an enormous variety of therapy practice, and training and supervision experience (see below), we have in common that we operate from a basis in systemic understanding. Our experience has been that the systemic paradigm has allowed us as clients and therapists, as trainers and supervisors, and as consultants to many different kinds of teams and organisations, to comfortably transfer our learning between these contexts. So whatever your own frameworks of understanding and practice, we have been determined to take our most successful PPD experiences into the most useful and generally applicable form that we can. We also have a small agenda of hoping that our readers will experience the benefits of consistency in systemic thinking.

Why we wanted to write this book together

We are a group of friends and colleagues who have known each other for many years and who work together often. We have provided personal and professional development training (PPD) in a range of counselling and psychotherapy contexts. We are based in different countries, including the UK, Ireland, Norway and The Netherlands, and we work and have learned from practices in other countries, such as Greece, Italy, Finland, Malta, Spain, Romania, Iceland, Germany, Turkey, Serbia, Bulgaria, Macedonia, Croatia, Hungary and Cyprus. We are trainers, supervisors, practitioners and supervisees, and sometimes still we inhabit the role of trainee. We share the view that training, supervision and therapeutic practice are connected through the processes of learning and development, often encapsulated in our PPD activity. Our shared systemic paradigm allows us to understand and enjoy complexity so that we may work with the complexity afforded by our multiple roles. Furthermore, we share a commitment to *enhancing* practice, at all levels of experience and across all the above roles of trainer, trainee, supervisor, supervisee and practitioner. Each chapter in this book will reflect some aspect of all these positions. Thus, we see PPD as a unifying and integral process in our collective development.

Exercise: What is the meaning of (PPD in your) life?

In keeping with the approaches that unfold in the book, we would like to invite you to step back from your eager process through this chapter and examine the assumptions that you generally apply to PPD. Please come with us through the following steps:

1   Please write down the very first thoughts that come to mind to describe your feelings as you approach PPD.
2   Now write a brief statement about the last PPD event or process that you were part of.
3   Try to imagine a consultant who was looking for indications in your reports of beliefs, attitudes and assumptions that have the potential to limit your PPD operations.
4   Imagine a friendly colleague was encouraging you to be much more constructive about your PPD experiences. What might they say? Write their wise and positive thoughts down.
5   Finally, comparing 3 and 4, write down what for you would be the best possible outcomes from working with this book. You might want to return to and expand this list as you proceed through the book.

What informs our philosophy of PPD?

Our approach to PPD is informed by systemic principles that help us integrate and unify our experiences of learning, development and improvement in the multiple professional roles we inhabit. In this section, we shall outline some of the systemic ideas that underpin the writing in the following chapters.

All the authors work with the central idea that the therapist is part of the therapeutic system, and by definition all roles of supervisor, supervisee, trainee and trainer form part of a complex interconnected system of influence, concern and mutual help. People's distress, dilemmas and struggles are viewed in the same way as their joys, strengths and triumphs – influencing and influenced by the ecosystem of interpersonal relationships within which we live our lives. We see this as a process of working 'within' and 'between' (i.e. exploring how the experiences of the individual are interacting with the relational in overlapping contexts that can support change, inhibit change and help create meanings at different levels of experience and relationship). We are interested in inter-generational learning in relational systems and how experiences with difference and diversity inform our positioning. In our work, we identify and track unhelpful patterns of interaction that people wish to change so that we might support and promote more satisfying relational experiences. This involves naming and exploring the connections between thought, emotion, intention, action and consequences in their recursive loops of communication. This attention to pattern and process, and context and meaning, in many ways defines systemic practice. Sometimes, we have been called process consultants in recognition of our curiosity about the connections between content and process in every significant rela-tionship. Within this framework, learning is based in good listening, and is seen as a co-constructed experience that co-evolves over time. Learning has the potential to be transformational, and to promote reflection, reflexivity, trust and effective problem-solving that is capable of creating new possibilities for practice and for life. In this book, we promote a relational, dialogical view of learning because in our experience, PPD becomes part of the self, and is shared in a forward-moving process of giving back. As one perspective on your own history of relational learning, we invite you into our second exercise.

Exercise: Your professional genogram

Gaining a deeper understanding of the many current and historical influences that have shaped the unique counsellors and psychotherapists we are becoming is a central element in the ongoing PPD of all of us – no matter what place we now occupy within our professions. We have made a short version of an exercise first developed by Magnuson (2000) as a way of inviting you, the readers, to become more actively involved in planning aspects of your own PPD through first locating yourself within the historical thread of the significant supervisor/mentor relationships, theoretical and social/political perspectives that have shaped your professional development.

For many years, family therapists have used a tool called the family genogram (McGoldrick and Gerson 1985) as a way of helping couples and families examine the relational patterns and historical events that have shaped their family and constructed its thematic struggles over time. The professional genogram is a way of making a similar type of examination of the multiplicity of relational, theoretical and other factors that shape a professional's approach to their practice over time.

The exercise can be done with different levels of detail, and we suggest that if you have not done this exercise before, you limit yourself in the first instance to including just the more obvious and central elements/persons in the genogram. You will find that as you do the exercise, you will begin to remember more of your own professional history and the relationships that were central to it. You will also begin to ask more complex questions concerning the relationship between different levels of the genogram.

The exercise involves mapping three levels of data with some straight lines drawing the connections between elements at different levels. The exercise comes in two parts. The first relates to the mapping/drawing of the professional genogram; the second concerns a space of reflective questioning and note-taking as you stand back and observe your own professional genogram.

Part I: Drawing the professional genogram

(a) Across the bottom of the page – from left to right and in historical sequence – put down the names of the key professional mentors, educators and supervisors who have influenced your professional development from the time you started your professional education until now. Under each name, put the year that your relationship commenced with this person and a single word or phrase that might represent something significant that you learned for your practice through this relationship. An example of an entry on this level of the genogram might be: Sally, 1994, projective identification. This bottom level of the genogram is completed by placing your own name in the middle of the page underneath all these other names and with a series of lines connecting you to each of the names.

(b) At the top level of the genogram going from left to right, put in sequence the names of the key theoreticians and master practitioners who have shaped your thinking and practice over time. Unlike the bottom level, which signifies real personal/professional relationships, this level will mostly refer to theoreticians/practitioners you have 'known' through their publications or perhaps through their videotapes or workshops and conferences. Examples of some entries on this level might be: C. Jung; I. Yalom; M. White. If you became acquainted with any of these masters/theoreticians through one of your supervisory/mentor relationships, draw a line in the genogram connecting the theoretician and supervisor.

(c) In the middle level of the genogram going from left to right, put the names of influences and general perspectives that shaped your understanding of yourself as a human being and your relationship to the world around you. Examples of entries at this level might be: Buddhism; Feminism; Social Justice; Ecology. If you were introduced to these influences through a relationship with either a mentor or a theoretician, draw a line connecting the perspective to that name on the genogram.

Part II: Observing the genogram and reflecting upon professional ancestry

Stand back and consider the professional ancestry you have just mapped. What do you notice about it? Are there some areas of your history that are richly connected to certain themes? Are there any voids or gaps in the whole picture that now 'appear'? What possibilities do you now see for further new or different activities that might enrich your PPD? Are there parts of your professional ancestry with which you might now like to re-engage in a deeper way? Make some notes for yourself arising from these and other reflections. You might consider sharing your reflections with a supervisor, a friend or the cat!

What to expect from the chapters in this book

Our book offers a rich variety of perspectives on, aspects of, and practical guidance for, PPD. Apart from cross-references that you will find within the chapters, it might help your orientation to be alert to five themes that are used in a variety of ways in different chapters. In our concluding chapter, we revisit these themes to draw your attention to some of the ways that they have been used most explicitly.

1   We have a continuing focus on the self of the practitioner. We conceptualise the processes we describe as developing both the personal and the professional selves of trainees, practitioners and supervisors. We find it useful to think of every interaction as creating new possibilities (i.e. new possible selves) of all concerned.
2   Supervision is a context of caring. Every chapter offers positive ways of attending to the needs and the intellectual and emotional development of therapists. Beyond this thread, there is an underlying and at times explicit theme of the importance for all practitioners, supervisors and therapists to take care of their own well-being.
3   We have considered in various ways the patterns that connect narratives from our PPD practices and how these have contributed to our development. PPD must always find connections between the therapist's personal and private life and their narratives of therapy practice. We hope that the experience of this book will provide readers with a basis for achieving coherence of their own personal and professional narratives.
4   We like to think that for all of us authors, the processes in creating this book have involved continuous reflection and reflexivity. You will find examples throughout the book of ways of achieving and maintaining an equable space for yourself and your supervisees. Such space is essential for establishing the conditions for productive reflection on practice and reflexively co-creating better understandings of the PPD processes themselves.
5   Our fifth position is to remember that all training is a process of learning. In places, you are invited into an explicit consideration of your assumptions

about how you and other adults learn. But every chapter invites you into your own learning processes with a reflexive follow-through to the learning of your trainees and you and their clients.

How to use this book

It is our hope that you will use this book in many ways. Although we have constructed the book as a coherent sequence, you may well have different ideas about what will be most functional for you. The book has been written for trainers and trainees, for supervisors and supervisees, and for practitioners across the range of counselling and psychotherapy approaches. We draw on tools, techniques and interventions that are common to all approaches and some that are more specific to systemic practice. We hope to be inclusive in our wish to show how systemic thinking can enhance learning and practice for us all. Each chapter offers challenges and possible solutions for different aspects of your PPD work. One suggestion could be that you scan the contents and choose an entry point that offers a manageable degree of challenge for you – between boredom and anxiety, as it has been described by Csikszentmihalyi (2000).

The book could be used as a module on a supervisor or practitioner training programme. It could be a continuing resource as your PPD unfolds. We hope you will be able to extract many different kinds of material to use in supporting the development of your colleagues. Perhaps it might even become a familiar resource that you will return to for different readings as you progress with your profession. The book contains a range of activities and exercises that are adaptable across a range of settings. We hope you enjoy it.

References

Csikszentmihalyi, M. (2000) *Beyond Boredom and Anxiety*, Boston, MA: Jossey-Bass.
McGoldrick, M. and Gerson, R. (1985) *Genograms in Family Assessment*, New York: W.W. Norton & Company.
Magnuson, S. (2000) 'The professional genogram: enhancing professional identity and clarity', *The Family Journal: Counselling and Therapy for Couples and Families*, 8: 399–401.

Chapter 2

PPD as processes of learning that enable the practitioner to create a self that is equipped for higher levels of professional mastery

Peter Stratton and Helga Hanks

This chapter offers a perspective that all forms of training and personal professional development (PPD) are fundamentally learning. Theories of adult learning converge towards an agreement that learning is achieved through active processes of various kinds. Being consistent with this view and because this book is a resource for the PPD of you, the readers, we make a number of offers of exercises by which you can choose to engage with the material. But these are just examples. The chapter will be of much greater value to you if you alight on ideas that could have direct application in your own context, and engage in a dialogue about them, either between yourself and your notes, or preferably by setting up a context in which you can explore them with one of more colleagues. Failing these possibilities, we know therapists who have successfully adapted ideas for their own use by explaining how they will use them to their cat.

Since you are reading this book, you are hoping to learn from it. Can we invite you to pause and examine what assumptions you have made about how that learning will take place?

*　*　*

Did you pause? Because this chapter provides some groundwork for tackling the various aspects of PPD, it provides plenty of invitations to work actively on the material. We, Peter and Helga, have shared many forms of PPD, including brief courses to expand the capabilities of various professionals; training in systemic psychotherapy up to accredited qualifying level; live supervision of clinical practice both in training courses and of individuals and teams in health service practice; and workshops of many kinds in varied contexts as part of continuing professional development. So the exercises in this chapter can be seen as examples of our PPD practices. When we offer material that is specific to Peter, particularly his more recent PPD activities, we use the verb 'I' (see the quotation from Grayson Perry on p. 25).

We are hoping this chapter will offer moderate, but not uncomfortable, challenges that will add to your ideas about learning in PPD. Let us start with a summary of some of the ideas that we will be elaborating.

Maybe you could notice what you expect to be doing to turn the information in the chapter from 'declarative' knowledge to 'procedural' knowledge: using it to change your practice.

Another reflective angel is to see whether you have applied your beliefs about how your students learn to an understanding of how you learned about their learning. (PS says: I know I typed 'angel' instead of 'angle', but the metaphor of taking a view from a higher (systemic folk say 'meta-') position seemed worth preserving.)

You approached this chapter with some expectations about what it would be, and how you might make use of having read it. The concept of the 'hermeneutic circle' (described below) deals with how much we insist on our pre-understandings and how much we are open to novelty. Therapeutically, we use an idea of being irreverent to our expectations so that we do not slip into unquestioned assumptions about the clients we see, which helps us maintain an active curiosity about them. From there, we can help the clients towards a similar stance with a core objective that they become aware of, interested in and able to use, an increased range of possibilities. Our hope is that you will encounter similar effects as you work through this chapter.

The chapter is oriented towards actively and creatively processing the material it presents. For this reason, there are many places headed 'Exercise' where you are invited to pause and engage in the specified activity. You may choose just to read on, but a metaphor I use in training is that you might be able to talk about Thailand by reading a guidebook rather than making the effort of actually going there. But the experience will not be the same, especially in terms of giving you opportunities to change.

The role of PPD in increasing the effectiveness of therapists

Exercise: The purpose of PPD

How would you rate the following statements about the main purpose of PPD? It is primarily:

1   For the practitioner to maintain the level of knowledge and expertise that they achieved at the end of training.
2   To troubleshoot particular difficulties in their practice as these arise.
3   To make good use of current experience and new ideas to keep practitioners at the upper end of their functioning.
4   To achieve a step change from acceptable competence to a higher level of mastery.

The fourth option may have struck you as overambitious (i.e. unrealistic). But this book is written to offer ways of going beyond routine maintenance. If we aspire to option 4, then significant learning is required. This chapter offers a variety of principles to support and expand the opportunities that learning research can offer to make training and PPD more powerful. The form of implementation will depend on the persons involved, the context and requirements, and what limits each puts on their aspirations. So this chapter is a buffet, not a set menu (buffet as in an array of food to choose from, not an aggressive shove), and our hope is that everyone will discover new dishes that they would like to try, including around use of metaphor.

There is a lot of emphasis on deutero-learning, as described by Gregory Bateson (1972), also known as learning how to learn, and, in management, second loop learning.

Our approaches to PPD have taken their basis in the work by Schön (1990) and others on the requirements of adult learning (Stratton 2005). But questions have been raised about whether the earlier work on reflective learning has merely been about maintaining an adequate level of competence and not the need for continuous personal development that would extend basic competences: "One of the gaps in Schön's work is a lack of comprehensive conceptualisation of the process of how experienced practitioners, who are expert in a particular practice, acquire new professional knowledge" (Sung-Chan 2000: 17).

Ericsson *et al.* (2006) elaborated:

> There are several factors that influence the level of professional achievement. First and foremost, extensive experience of activities in a domain is necessary to reach very high levels of performance. Extensive experience in a domain does not, however, invariably lead to expert levels of achievement. When individuals are first introduced to a professional domain after completing their basic training and formal education, they often work as apprentices and are supervised by more-experienced professionals as they accomplish their work-related responsibilities. After months of experience they typically attain an acceptable level of proficiency, and with longer experience, often years, they are able to work as independent professionals. At that time, most professionals reach a stable, average level of performance, and then they maintain this pedestrian level for the rest of their careers. In contrast, some continue to improve and eventually reach the highest levels of professional mastery.
>
> (p. 685)

As we start to approach this goal, we perhaps need to get free of some powerfully driven beliefs in our society in relation to mental health. If our conceptualisation of best practice is of a search for the clearest possible formulation of the client's problem and then applying the most effective treatment of that problem, then all of purposes 1, 2 and 3 will apply. But research has demonstrated that some therapists are consistently much more effective than the average. What makes the difference? Some clues come from current questioning of the assumptions built into a diagnosis-treatment model, and in particular the assumptions underlying dominant approaches in mental health. Epstein *et al.* (2013) place the approach of the Diagnostic and Statistical Manual (DSM-5) within what we would call 'essentialising': the attribution of a person's way of being to a built-in characteristic such as a fixed personality or genetic inheritance. While we and our clients are constrained to work in health systems that prescribe therapies and evaluate effectiveness in terms of the DSM approach, it requires constant vigilance to avoid talking and thinking in these terms. As Epstein *et al.* (2013) say:

> It is the authors' collective experience that the numbers of clients who bring self-descriptions heavily laden with psychiatric and psychological terms and jargon to the therapeutic encounter, have increased enormously. What are the consequences of these self-descriptions for our notions of the self and for society? Recent research in the fields of psycholinguistics, language, psychology, sociology, philosophy and cultural studies, all point towards the many ways in which language and our ways of using language influence our ways of living as well as our constructions of self.
>
> (p. 157)

It has been a staple of our training at all levels to create games in which explaining by using nouns is constantly challenged. Furman and Ahola's (1992) brilliant metaphor was that if a psychiatrist wants to steal autonomy from a patient, they are in the position of a pickpocket in a nudist camp. First you have to sew pockets, or psychiatric labels, on to the person, then you can proceed to steal from them. We might have trainees in pairs, one describing their client and the second picking up every time an intrinsic property of the person was stated or implied, so the two could work together to make it less a description of a kind of person. 'An aggressive man' is clearly problematic for introducing change. But even 'he became aggressive' locates the aggression inside the person. A much more detailed approach is provided by analysing the forms of attributions by which people explain and predict (Bradbury and Fincham 1990). This is one area in which our research into family therapy sessions (Stratton *et al.* 1986) became a foundation for aspects of the therapy, training and PPD that have been provided by the Leeds Family Therapy Research Centre (LFTRC) (Stratton 2003a, 2003b). See also Chapter 3, 'Attributions in clinical settings', in Munton *et al.* (1999).

Exercise: Avoiding labelling

You are supervising a group of trainee therapists. They start presenting work with a client who is a depressive. Can you describe alternative ways of talking about this person by which you might gently lead them towards conversations that will give them more therapeutic leverage?

In such discussions, there may be progression from 'a depressive' through talk of experiencing depressed feeling, to describing the experience as one that I interpret as having features in common with those of other people who have been described as depressed.

What understandings might you build from the following statements based on Kogan and Gale (1997)?

- Self is not a social product, but a social accomplishment.
- Personal identity is an activity, rather than a thing.
- Context is not a bucket, but a performance: we accomplish who we are and what we are on an ongoing basis through interpretive practices.

Approaches to increasing effectiveness

Coming back to the challenge of using PPD to raise practice above its current level, I would also come back to the limited aspiration represented by attempts to demand a standard approach. Greenhalgh *et al.* (2014), writing in the *BMJ* on the topic 'Evidence based medicine: a movement in crisis?', propose that expert practice is a matter of judgement, not of following rules, even if these are prescribed by the evidence base:

> Real evidence based medicine is not bound by rules. The Dreyfus brothers (Dreyfus and Dreyfus 1987) have described five levels of learning, beginning with the novice who learns the basic rules and applies them mechanically with no attention to context. The next two stages involve increasing depth of knowledge and sensitivity to context when applying rules. In the fourth and fifth stages, rule following gives way to expert judgments, characterised by rapid, intuitive reasoning informed by imagination, common sense, and judiciously selected research evidence and other rules.
>
> (pp. 42–3)

In clinical diagnosis, for example, the novice clinician works methodically and slowly through a long and standardised history, exhaustive physical examination, and (often numerous) diagnostic tests. The expert, in contrast, makes a rapid initial differential diagnosis through intuition, then uses a more selective history, examination, and set of tests to rule in or rule out particular possibilities. To equate 'quality' in clinical care with strict adherence to guidelines or protocols, however robust these rules may be, is to overlook the evidence on the more sophisticated process of advanced expertise.

(pp. 43–4)

While we are recognising the tendency for practitioners to remain at a 'pedestrian' level, we should also accept that training and supervision can also settle into a comfortable routine. We need to think about all possible ways of upgrading our supervisory practice if we are to provide PPD that will facilitate a parallel step change in standards of the participants.

Fortunately, many psychotherapy stances lend themselves to drawing in forms of training and learning that have been developed in various fields, integrating them into a coherent philosophy of PPD and then specifying them to be usable in any area of counselling and psychotherapy. This chapter concentrates on principles that are consistent with systemic thinking, but wherever possible bringing some news of difference from outside our own field.

Exercise: Raising your game

Please list some principles from your own approach to counselling or psychotherapy that might serve to lift your PPD to a new level.

Here are some from systemics. Try putting yours alongside and looking for useful connections:

- Meaning is dialogically constructed.
- Approaches that increase rather than close off options.
- Constant reflection on the processes of learning.
- Reflexive application.
- Application in practice to therapist-client relationships.
- Strengths orientation.
- Attention to the learner's self-narrative.

We each have our own version of each of these, but the multidisciplinary team at the LFTRC has always found it useful to draw on our backgrounds in other areas to enrich the systemic view. This wider perspective has been most useful because of the range of courses we provided for other professionals. When we created the qualifying training in 1995, we already had a history in Leeds of providing a systemic input in other contexts, from elective undergraduate courses on family systemics applied to child abuse through to broader systemic contributions to the clinical psychology training including a systemic approach to child development (Stratton 2003c). We regularly ran courses for social workers to incorporate systemic thinking more explicitly in their work. Then there has been the mission to bring news of systemics to other professions (e.g. speech therapists, residential care workers and a health service psychotherapy department).

In all such courses, we have tried for an ethos in which both the activities in the training and the stance of trainees and tutors exemplify the principles we were teaching, progressively introducing what were inevitably our favourite ideas at the time, but setting up exercises in which they could be built into the process and style, not just the content, of what was discussed or enacted. This range of experiences in training, in addition to what we were undertaking within the clinic, formed what we felt was well-tested material for training presented in the LFTRC book *Family Therapy: Training and Practice* (Stratton *et al.* 1990). One aspect of our experiences that formed the style of the book was to continuously invite the readers into prescribed activities that we hoped would enable them to integrate the material into their professional self, not merely reading a set of techniques to apply to their clients. What we said then in the chapter on supervision (which drew heavily on Liddle *et al.* 1988) about the reasons that supervision is not just useful, but essential, still seems relevant. We grouped the reasons under four headings of systemic significance (pp. 96–9):

(a) dynamics within practitioners;
(b) dynamics of the work;
(c) the complexity of the work; and
(d) dynamics within teams.

This book invites you to open yourself to change through the ideas offered about PPD. One aid to such processes can come from drawing on research into creativity.

Creativity

An area in which the author has provided many workshops and conference presentations is that of creativity. As in other areas, for our purposes, we need to break away from the tendency to see creativity as a function, or even a measurable capacity, of an individual person. Those positions have been productive but we will be more interested in the processes between people by which novel meanings are created. It is almost a definition of psychotherapy that an end result should be understandings and abilities to act that were not previously available. And to foster creativity in clients requires creativity in the therapist, as well as in their trainers and supervisors. Bateson (1972) proposed that advances in scientific thought come from a combination of loose and strict thinking, and he saw this combination as the most precious tool of science. Sometimes, training, with its requirement to demonstrate acceptable competence, can overemphasise strict thinking. One set of exercises we have used is around encouraging habitual use of metaphor, which is one route to creating space free from strict seriousness.

Exercise: Using metaphors in different ways

Set up two different chairs opposite each other. When you sit in one, you will enact a version of your self that is highly focused on improving your performance. When you move to the other chair, you are the more irreverent self that is determined to enjoy these exercises. Sit in each chair in turn, getting into that role. Now, moving rapidly between the two chairs/selves, have a discussion exploring one of the following metaphors in turn. What ideas does it potentiate? Where could its implications be misleading?

- Your professional development as running a small business such as a grocery store.
- A training course as crash-landing your spaceship on an unexplored planet.
- Therapists as comedians.
- Progress in your profession as a termite's nest.

Of course, you could do this exercise with colleagues, in which case our instruction has been, "In groups of three or four, have the most fun (wacky, uncritical, playful, ribald, energetic, irreverent, novel) discussion you can manage."

These ideas, and many more, are elaborated by Gareth Morgan (1993, 1997) from his work on organisations. When we are at ease with and alert to metaphor for ourselves, we will be likely to use them productively with clients (Cade 1995).

My approach to creativity has been that it is the default mode for humans. Eighteen-month-old children do not need training to be actively exploratory and creative; they just need to be free of stress. We should try to be more like them. But perhaps we not only have trouble getting free from stress, especially time pressure; we have also all found that strict, or convergent, thinking is generally extremely successful, so it becomes the default mode. What do you suggest we do about this? How about hanging a sign facing your therapist or supervisory chair saying:

"Relax, slow down, be creative"

The classic story of creativity is based on studies of major creative achievements, and is formulated as a process of preparation, incubation, inspiration and verification – useful concepts, but the most relevant for the everyday creativity that we need to be using all the time is of incubation. A review of research (Sio and Ormerod 2009) concluded that novel solutions do emerge after a period away from consciously thinking about the problem, but are less likely in conditions of high demand, or of no demand at all. This suggests that when feeling stuck in therapy, it would be effective to park the problem but maintain a manageable level of demand so that incubation can occur later. By the way, were you thinking there of the therapist? We can also be thinking in terms of the client's feeling of stress being maintained at an optimal level.

Exercise: Helping supervisees control their stress

Devise an exercise by which your supervisees can practise recognising and moderating their sense of the demands on them. What can they call on as a 'secure base' that will help them?

Keeping improvements, not deterioration, in fast competence

Our field has made good use of the idea of a progression from unconscious incompetence through conscious incompetence to conscious competence and finally unconscious competence. On reflection, this description is rather pejorative and linear. Sometimes, what you don't know does not hurt you. And unconscious competence might amount to 'fast thinking', as described by Daniel Kahneman (2012), who gives many examples of how it can be limiting and inimical to progress. In the form of 'prejudice' (Cecchin *et al.* 1994), it can begin to look like unconscious incompetence all over again.

We could instead describe a circular process:

1 Starting from unconsidered aspects of practising that may often (though probably not always) produce unfavourable results without really knowing why. Could also be described as *fast* thinking.
2 With training, one can be aware of why one is acting in this way. Training slows the process down so that it can be examined.
3 With effective training, one is able to practise, with slowed awareness, the activities that are likely to be effective.
4 With considerable experience, supported by PPD, these more effective practices become readily available without needing deliberation in the moment. This is what we could call unconsidered aspects of practising that very often (though probably not always) produce favourable results without really knowing why. They are characteristic of experienced and effective therapists.
5 Aspects of unconscious competence may not remain consistently effective as the therapist, their context and their clients change. If they become sometimes ineffective, we return to 1.

It seems plausible that an effective therapist defines their self-as-therapist primarily in terms of these fast/unconsidered/unconscious interventions. So supervision and PPD are needed to pull these unconscious practices back into

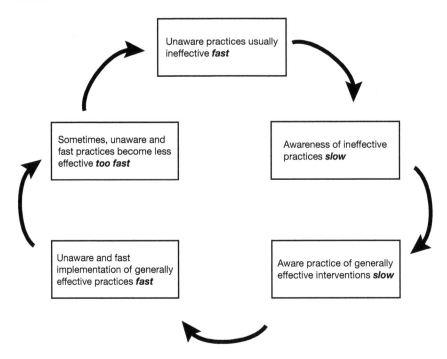

Figure 2.1 Cycle of progression from 'unconscious incompetence' to unconscious competence, and sometimes back to incompetence

consciousness to check that they have not lost their effectiveness. It is also useful for the supervisor to gain a better understanding of how the effective therapists arrive at their better interventions. The final deterioration is avoided through reflective consideration of one's own processes, reflexive checking out in context so that you have a higher level of understanding of your own learning processes.

Of course, a true circle does not have a starting point. We need to be alert to the fact that all trainees and therapists come to us being at different points on the circle for different aspects of their practice.

In different ways, all of the suggestions so far have been about the learning of the therapist and sometimes of the trainer/supervisor. Our next step is an explicit consideration of processes of adult learning.

Autonomous and reflexive adult learning

Exercise: What kind of teaching is more effective?

If Group A students are taught by lectures from a highly skilled and highly rated lecturer, and for Group B an inexperienced instructor used exploratory methods derived from psychological research, which of the following would you expect to be the outcome?

1   Group B enjoyed the teaching more but learned less.
2   Group A had better attendance.
3   Group B had better attendance and was more engaged.
4   Group B achieved more than twice the learning of Group A.

Although in a different context, the comparison of two different approaches to teaching by Deslauriers *et al.* (2011) achieved results that are illustrative of the outcomes that our active autonomous learning (Stratton 2005) was designed to achieve:

> to have the students spend all their time in class engaged in deliberate practice at 'thinking scientifically' in the form of making and testing predictions and arguments about the relevant topics, solving problems, and critiquing their own reasoning and that of others.
>
> Deslauriers *et al.* (2011: 862)

The outcome of the Deslauriers study?

> We measured the learning of a specific set of topics and objectives when taught by 3 hours of traditional lecture given by an experienced highly rated instructor and 3 hours of instruction given by a trained but inexperienced instructor using instruction based on research in cognitive psychology and physics education. The comparison was made between two large sections ($N = 267$ and $N = 271$) of an introductory undergraduate physics course. We found increased student attendance, higher engagement, and more than twice the learning in the section taught using research-based instruction.
>
> (p. 862)

This kind of finding suggests that the style of instruction has a significant effect on the quality of learning. But our approach has particularly been in terms of the processes by which adults learn. Our initial model was derived primarily from the work of educationalists such as Schön (1990), Kolb (1983) and Gibbs (1994). It is described in some detail by Stratton (2005), and in that article considerable effort went into progressively building the model while encouraging the reader to reflexively apply their developing understanding to the processes described in the model. In that way, the model would become a creator and describer of their experience and hopefully thereby become embedded in their approach to new learning experiences.

The Leeds Family Therapy Research Centre (LFTRC) learning spiral

In this chapter, it is not realistic or appropriate to repeat the process by which we led the reader through the spiral, but you are warmly invited to return to the original article to obtain a more complete understanding than is possible here. In summary, the spiral starts with an acceptance that a training or PPD process usually starts with an external source of information. Please trace the following thoughts through the progression of the spiral in Figure 2.3.

The concept of the hermeneutic circle (Figure 2.2) gives us a concrete way of thinking about how this information will be processed through the therapist's existing structures of meaning and will then be subjected to dialogue either with others or within the self. Refer to Sheehan (Chapter 8, this volume) for a more comprehensive account of Ricoeur's hermeneutics.

As the transformed information becomes part of the self of the therapist, it will be incorporated into aspects of practice, and so become selectively meaningful in relation to the contexts of practice. To be less abstract, when an idea that was sparked by a supervisor is eventually tried at the next session with the Smiths, it will be formed in terms of the supervisory experience. For the therapist's learning to progress, there are then three processes that might be undertaken. They may reflect on how they operated this particular process of learning that could give them a greater insight about themselves as a learner. They are likely to monitor the effects of the supervisor's intervention on their practice. And they may articulate their understanding whether in a group discussion, by writing notes or

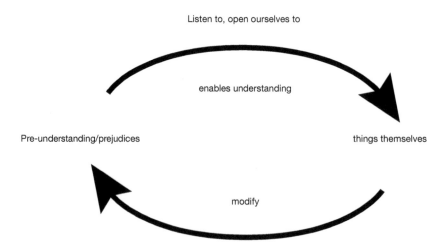

Listen to, open ourselves to

enables understanding

Pre-understanding/prejudices

things themselves

modify

Figure 2.2 The hermeneutic circle (Gadamer's version)

as an internal dialogue. The progressive reflections that arise as these forms of enhanced awareness are undertaken lead to an achievement that is summarised in the model as a 'deep learning of theory'. Then, as it is put in the Stratton (2005) article, "when they are sitting with the Smith parents who have reverted to trading insults, they will be able to interrogate their theory and generate ideas of how to go on" (p. 232).

A couple of cautionary comments. As discussed in the original article, Figure 2.3 is not actually a spiral, and it is drawn as a linear progression. If you wish, you can overcome these concerns by drawing upward arrows showing the implications that arise from activities at each level for the levels above. (I have tried this but found the resulting image too complicated to print, but please have a go.)

Second, the spiral is not prescribed as a definitive statement of the forms and stages through which learning must proceed. It is one formulation, based on an extensive literature, but only used here so that we have a concrete example on which to work. As we progress, you may wish to create your own diagram of a learning process that fits better with your style and objectives.

Since the years during which the learning spiral was developed, there have been a number of developments that can contribute to our understanding of how PPD can operate for the most effective learning. In this chapter, several exercises are offered by which you can use the structure of the spiral to consolidate your ideas.

Exercise: Enacting the learning spiral to create your own meanings for it

An exercise that I have used in workshops for trainers on learning is to offer a skeleton of Figure 2.3 and invite participants, in groups of about three, to fill in the content. The idea is that they will make the understanding of the spiral their own by enacting the reflections and articulations in dialogue. So you are invited to take the skeleton in Figure 2.4 and propose descriptions for content as further ideas are offered in the next few pages. Participants have found this task demanding but rewarding, even when it could not be fully completed within the workshop. Using this book means that you will have more time so you could add a further element, consistent with the model, of monitoring your learning about learning while you struggle (hopefully not on your own) with the exercise.

Concretely, I would suggest that you make copies of this 'skeleton spiral' to complete in your own terms. First, so that your learning is taking place with reference to its context, and by referring back to the original spiral, fill in descriptions of your learning from the content to this chapter. Later, you could take other copies as a framework for planning learning for others.

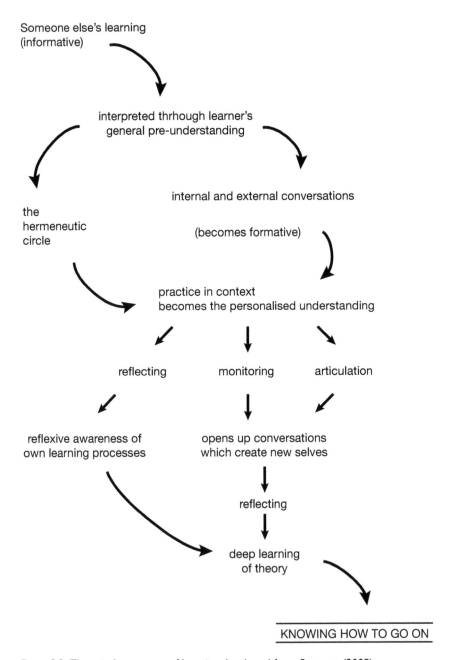

Someone else's learning
(informative)

interpreted thrhough learner's
general pre-understanding

internal and external conversations

the
hermeneutic
circle

(becomes formative)

practice in context
becomes the personalised understanding

reflecting   monitoring   articulation

reflexive awareness of   opens up conversations
own learning processes   which create new selves

reflecting

deep learning
of theory

KNOWING HOW TO GO ON

Figure 2.3 The spiral processes of learning developed from Stratton (2005)

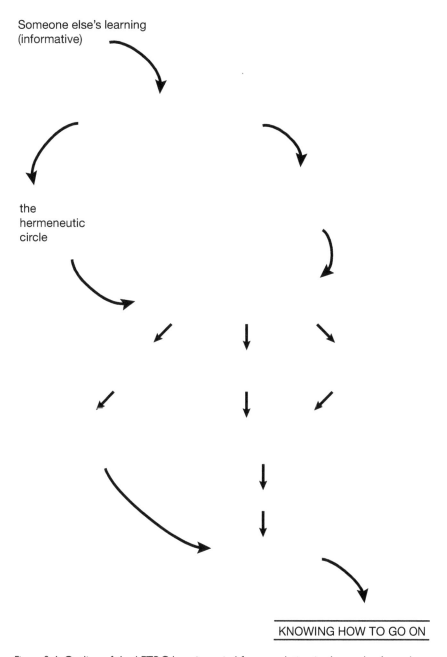

Someone else's learning
(informative)

the
hermeneutic
circle

KNOWING HOW TO GO ON

Figure 2.4 Outline of the LFTRC learning spiral for completion in the readers' words

As new approaches to systemic therapy have developed, so innovations in PPD can be based on them. For example, De Jong and Berg (2011) built on the proposals of Steiner *et al.* (1999) to create a programme of learning interview skills through a solution focus approach. They summarise Steiner as:

> Steiner *et al.* (1999) emphasized that positive interdependence among participant learners, face-to-face interaction, individual accountability and personal responsibility, social skills, and group evaluation of learning goals all are critical to effective learning. The students also seem to echo Steiner *et al.*'s (1999) list of skills fostered by collaborative learning. These include relationship building, small-group skills, effective communication among participants, problem solving and creativity, influencing one another, and critical thinking.
>
> (p. 34)

In training and supervision for PPD, we look for an understanding of learning that is specifically relevant for experienced adults. It is my experience, as described by others, that most students up to doctoral level and beyond rely on the learning strategies that they developed at the start of secondary schooling aged around 12 years. It is in educational research and theorising that the needs of adult learners have been explicitly considered.

Supervised therapy as action research

It can be useful to think of therapy as action research in which the researcher (but we can think of the therapist and the supervisor) actively participates in the situation that they are researching. The ideas of participatory action research connect the conceptualisation of learning in this chapter with a major movement in societal research. In this tradition, research is conducted in the process of actively bringing about change, "learning to do it by doing it" (Freire 1982). In this sense, therapy can be understood as research in which the therapist is not a puppeteer pulling the strings, but a full participant in a joint process of struggle to discover what happens when therapeutic principles are applied to the situation of the client.

A comparatively recent development that originated in language teaching has interesting correspondences with systemic principles. Exploratory practice (EP) (Allwright and Hanks 2009) proposes a stance of teachers and students as co-researchers with an orientation to puzzlement rather than problem-solving (see especially Chapters 5 and 10). We see correspondences with a stance of curiosity and a parallel with the claim in systemics that therapy creates change in the therapist and works through that change being encountered by the family.

A further connection is provided by Tajino and Smith (2005), elaborating EP through soft systems methodology (SSM):

Unlike typical 'hard' systems approaches which have been developed in natural sciences to solve problems involving clear cause-effect relationships, SSM is a 'soft' systems approach that deals with complex human situations in which people with various world views, or senses of values, are engaged in communication.

(p. 448)

SSM would certainly seem to apply to family therapy contexts when seen from the perspective of SFT when it rejects the attempt of DSM to provide a highly specified problem definition. We encountered SSM in the context of creative organisational management (Flood and Jackson 1991), but so far as I know it has never been explored in SFT, and I mention it here, along with exploratory practice, as a so far untapped resource rather than something we have experience of using in PPD.

Educational thinking has moved beyond the concepts of reflective practice introduced by Schön. Bradbury *et al.* (2010) introduce their book as follows: "*Beyond Reflective Practice* examines what new forms of professional reflective practice are emerging. It examines in particular the relationships between reflective practitioners and those upon whom they practise."

Meanwhile, family therapy has moved to a more explicit focus on language. A clear statement of the senses in which language shapes identities is provided by Epstein *et al.* (2013), while arguing that the Diagnostic and Statistical Manual (DSM) is destructive in its effects of channelling concepts of self into predefined and homogeneous psychiatric definitions. They quote Harry Goolishian (1990):

The transformational power of narrative rests in its capacity to re-relate the events of our lives in the context of new and different meaning. We live in and through the narrative identities that we develop in conversation with each other. The skill of the therapist is the expertise to participate in this process.

(Epstein *et al.* 2013: 164)

Such sources have combined with the thinking in terms of dialogical construction of selves to move us towards thinking consistently in terms of the essential role of dialogue in learning.

Training and PPD as constructing new selves and making them available in the practice

If training and PPD are constructed with a total focus on the practitioner, then they must be framed in terms of the self of that practitioner. But systemics adds the recognition that in training, just as in therapy, the person who is most readily changed is the (self of the) therapist/trainer.

An objective of training that needs to be supported by PPD is to undo any separation between the systemic self that operates during therapy and the selves operating in external life. Simon (2006) argues that research points to the value of the therapist's world view matching that of the therapy model they are using. He in fact sees it as helping to resolve the dispute between common factors and model-specific theories: "This article has proposed that the way to advance the common factors/model-specific factors dialogue beyond its current dissatisfying state is to install the self of the therapist at the center of the discussion" (p. 343).

Simon's (2006) section 'Implications for training' proposes having trainees work to define their world view by, among other things, interrogating their life decisions and life structures "with an eye toward discerning the worldview that informs them" (p. 341). However, Simon presents the trainee world view as fixed and just needing to be discovered so that they can be presented with an array of therapies in order to choose the one that most closely matches. But our experience is that the world view can be profoundly affected by their experience of the therapy in which they train. Personal therapy in psychodynamics is not just the avowed matter of self-understanding; it is also an experience designed to convert them towards the world view of the particular form of psychoanalytic theory on which their training is based. So when systemic training is invited to show how the effects of a personal therapy are achieved, it is not just a matter of achieving the needed forms and levels of self-understanding. It is also a challenge to show how our methods produce a personal development that incorporates the world view of the model.

The study of human development across the lifespan has learning at its core. But we need to break away from the exclusive focus on processes within the individual that dominates the psychological literature. One route to this for me has been the move away from fixed concepts of self. Early reviews (Markus and Nurius 1986; Markus and Wurf 1987) established the value of thinking in terms of multiple selves, and LFTRC took this up in terms of nested models of self and others (Stratton *et al.* 1993). This approach gave a language to the ways the self is constituted by the changing images of others, of the person's relationships and their representation of their self. As they act out from these nested conceptualisations, they create change in those with whom they are interacting and so create a new version of their self.

How are we to talk of 'the self' when such discourse can approach the kind of reification that has become distinctly unfashionable in social constructionist systemic therapy? Martin and Sugarman (2001: 104) proposed that the self be seen to exist as a "particular kind of reflective, interpretive understanding – an understanding that is always embodied and unfolding within an historical, sociocultural tradition of living (a life world)." In other words, the self as 'embodied understanding', a position that Smith (2014: 35) suggests combines, or bridges, "social constructionism" with "irreducible agency."

So PPD would then work towards matching the therapist's understanding of their self-as-therapist with their understanding of the model of therapy they are offering. This requires either or both of supporting trainees (or course applicants) to find the model that fits best for them, while encouraging them to build their chosen model into their full world view (i.e. their self in all contexts, not just the therapy situation). The LFTRC has extensive experience of providing four- or six-day courses that provide basic systemic methods but also encourage a wholesale adoption of a systemic world view. Our experience has been that a substantial proportion of the professionals report after the course that it changed their whole approach to how they worked. Some trained and experienced professionals are able to readily take on the fundamental mind set of systemics and build it into their sense of professional self. The reciprocal experience is that even after a four-year training, some graduates of a systemic therapy course readily return to the professional styles that they had developed before entering the training.

Rober (2005) explores the dialogical self of the therapist as being continually constructed through inner dialogue. Drawing on Bakhtin and Volosinov, he describes the self as a dialogue of multiple inner voices. It was Hermans *et al.* (1992) who elaborated the idea of multiple selves being constructed in dialogue with others.

Dialogical construction of selves

'I' is a verb masquerading as a noun.

Julian Baggini, quoted by Grayson Perry,
The Guardian, 4 October 2014

The adventure of moving beyond our sound but pedestrian level is easier if we recognise two things about our self: that self is an enactment and not a fixed object; and it could be useful to think that we can each create hundreds of different selves. Every day.

The formulation that now offers the most practicable way of discussing multiple selves is that of Hermans' theory of the dialogical construction of self (Hermans *et al.* 1992; Hermans and Hermans-Jansen 2003). This gives a concrete way of expanding our commitment to relational processes and applying it in PPD to expanding therapists' repertoires of self. It is currently being developed and elaborated for varied contexts, including "education and psychotherapy, multi-cultural identities, child-rearing practices, adult development, consumer behaviour, the use of the internet and the value of silence" (Hermans and Gieser 2011).

Dialogical construction of selves claims that new selves are created in each encounter. In supervision, that means that the supervisor is, whether or not explicitly, working to expand the repertoire of selves of the therapist in ways that will increase their effectiveness. When a trainer is working with a group to elaborate their self-definition to include some aspect of research competence, the relationship is less direct than individual supervision, but the objective is the same. The trainer has come by a belief (prejudice), perhaps that research-informed practice has certain advantages, and takes on the job of fostering an increased and informed engagement with research by the trainee.

Recently, Hermans (2014) offers a dialogical theory of counselling in which the self is considered as a mini-society of relatively autonomous I-positions that simultaneously function as part of the larger society.

In the wider field of systemic sciences, there are extensive discussions of the fluidity and in some senses stability of the self. Smith (2014) constructs a conceptual framework based in autopoeisis. Thinking about autopoeisis has developed considerably since the way Maturana's (2002) formulation has been taken up in systemic psychotherapy. Smith (2014) offers a detailed review of current approaches to the self-concept driven initially by his concern with teachers in training:

> The motivation to write this paper came from a need to review the extensive self-concept literature to apply the theory of possible selves to empirical research on the development of 'self-concept as a teacher' amongst beginning teachers. In that project, possible selves and LSDP offered structural interpretations and frameworks for understanding the process of change within the lifeworld and across the life span of beginning teachers.
>
> (p. 32)

In an indication of future possibilities in training opened up by a cyber-systemic course of adult reflexive learning, Ison and Blackmore (2014) describe a module developed for the UK Open University, Masters Program on Systems Thinking in Practice, a 'learning system for mature-age students'. The programme draws on the authors' experiences in reflective learning and communities of practice, and is conducted largely through activities such as online discussions and blogging. The success of these programs, which have a strong orientation to applicability, points to a future in which much PPD might be conducted remotely.

Implementation for fostering creativity and research training

PPD is about new understandings and practices, and so is fundamentally creative. But supervisors cannot easily be playful and creative all from their own resources and initiatives.

Exercise: Getting help for your creative supervision

Discuss how you would get your therapists to elicit greater creativity and a greater range of alternatives, from you, their supervisor.

What concepts of creativity did you start from that had an effect of limiting these ideas? Let's see if we can help.

We could, for example, consider the way that the whole system of anticipatory schemas is geared to minimising the exploratory cycle; to find a good enough match to an available schema so that the process of exploration can stop. Creativity is about finding ways to insist on continuation of the exploration by using curiosity to find unanswered questions.

Exercise: Keeping creative exploration going

What would stop premature closure in a discussion during supervision? And in the next session when the therapist is working without supervision?

As stated earlier, my approach to creativity is as an intrinsic human function. So our task is not to create or instil creativity, but to reduce the influence of factors that prevent its benefits. There is a substantial literature body of ideas from outside of psychotherapy that we can draw on. One theme has been on overcoming 'functional fixedness' (McCaffrey 2012). This area sees the main obstacle to creativity as being the way we readily perceive the function or purpose of anything we encounter, and that prevents a more fluid exploration of its potential. Carnevale (1998) discusses the problem as one of overcoming prototypes. The capacity to unlearn functional fixedness is especially relevant in this chapter, which is based on PPD experiences of cultivating the selves of the therapist that have more freedom to create the unexpected.

Epstein *et al.* (2013) quote Richard Rorty's (1989: 39–40) nicely systemic notion of intellectual playfulness:

> This playfulness is the product of their shared ability to appreciate the power of redescribing, the power of language to make new and different things possible and important – an appreciation which becomes possible only when one's aim becomes an expanding repertoire of alternative descriptions rather than The One Right description.

In Epstein *et al.*'s view, "The training of therapists would come to resemble more a comprehensive liberal arts education than training in a professional craft" (p. 164).

As an alternative, with a secure base being needed for playful (irreverent) exploration, research-based manuals specifically can contribute to this secure base (Stratton 2013). 'Research-based' means that the content of the manual has been the basis for therapies that were empirically shown to be effective. In a UK government project, a large team of therapists reviewed all of the existing research-based manuals in a variety of psychotherapies – cognitive, systemic, psycho-analytic and humanistic – in order to list the range of competences that had been reported (Pilling and Roth 2011). In the case of systemic therapies, this exercise identified 254 specific evidenced competences (Stratton *et al.* 2011). Systemic therapists could certainly regard this specification as indicating that they have a secure base from which to create an expanded repertoire.

A form of exercise by which PPD can create surprising possibilities

An exercise that I have used to cultivate a dialogically constructed self of trainees as competent researchers (Stratton 2007) brings together a number of the themes of this chapter.

Many students on family therapy training courses construe themselves as incapable of and repelled by research. With such a self-definition, it is difficult to engage with research, either in the form of research activity or of informed reading of research articles. This negativity is damaging to the profession if it carries through to an image that psychotherapy practice rejects and ignores research. Many trainers, with a similar experience in their own training, find it difficult to inspire their trainees to use research findings.

The context of the teaching was a session on social constructionism at the start of Year 4. A central role for the self of the therapist had been proposed based on Simon (2006). Trainees had completed a series of exercises around dialogue and self, of which the last, introduced in two parts, was to help them focus on how they constructed their own self as a systemic therapist:

> Write down a set of words that apply to your therapeutic self. Don't be constrained by modesty. Rather, take a meta-position of the kind of description that might be given by a client who really appreciates how you have been with them.
>
> Now discuss with a colleague how your self-definition relates to the model of therapy you are following at present.

At this point, the concept of multiple selves constructed within dialogue was introduced. Leading towards the research exercise, we explored the dialogical construction of selves during each conversation and each context. Following this preparation, the intervention made simple use of the context of the research training. In Year 3, all trainees had participated in a collaborative research project in the form of a Practitioner Research Network based on the SCORE measure of family functioning (Stratton 2007). All had engaged successfully with the project and had submitted an individual research report, in journal style, as part of the assessment. The exercise capitalised on their success by drawing attention to the fact that each had successfully functioned as a researcher. They were then invited to form pairs and conduct a dialogue for 10 minutes:

> Both take the role of a competent and confident researcher who has unlimited resources, and discuss ways in which you might take the SCORE research forward.

They were encouraged to exaggerate their portrayal of a researcher in order to construct that version of self as fully as possible.

A few trainees had difficulty in suspending their disbelief in themselves as researchers, but most reported that the exercise had been successful in helping them to enrich their self-description as being at ease with research. Much humour was evident in the discussion, apparently facilitated by the unrealistically unconstrained topic.

Exercise: Fostering new selves with a specific capability

Using the exercise just described as a model, choose an aspect of performance that you want to be able to foster in your provision of training or PPD. Devise a description of how you would apply this approach in your PPD to create new selves that have more capability to achieve that performance.

Back to the learning spiral

By this stage, you have been offered a variety of ideas, many from outside the contexts of therapy PPD, and have been invited to take them on through different kinds of active process.

Exercise: Completing the learning spiral with your own words

Take a copy of the skeleton model of Figure 2.4. With your colleague, if you have been working through this chapter with them, otherwise by activating a community of your relevant selves, discuss then fill in your own wordings for the headings in terms of your personal experience of this chapter so that you become an 'embodied understanding'.

Incubation alone may not be sufficient for this exercise. I would encourage you to scan back through the chapter to be reminded of all the good ideas you had while reading it.

Conclusion

This chapter has capitalised on the fact that working through the chapter is itself a learning experience. It has therefore been appropriate to recursively apply the ideas to your experience of the learning process itself. The intention has been to lead you into the creation of a newly constructed learning self, with a usable structure into which you can coordinate the content of successive chapters of this book.

Exercise: Starting your elaboration of the learning spiral for your own PPD

As a final exercise to make the most productive use of this chapter, take a copy of the skeleton spiral and write new entries of specific ways that these processes could be present in your main PPD activities. As you work through the remaining chapters of this book, you will find plenty of inspiration to elaborate these entries.

References

Allwright, D. and Hanks, J. (2009) *The Developing Language Learner: An Introduction to Exploratory Practice*, Basingstoke, UK: Palgrave Macmillan.

Bateson, G. (1972) *Steps to an Ecology of Mind*. New York: Ballentine.

Bradbury, H., Frost, N., Kilminster, S. and Zukas, M. (2010) *Beyond Reflective Practice: New Approaches to Professional Lifelong Learning*, London: Routledge.

Bradbury, T.N. and Fincham, F.D. (1990) 'Attribution in marriage: review and critique', *Psychological Bulletin*, 107: 3–33.

Cade, B. (1995) 'Treating the house like a hotel: from simile to metaphor', *Human Systems: The Journal of Systemic Consultation & Management*, 6: 279–94.

Carnevale, P.J. (1998) 'Social values and social conflict: creative problem solving and categorization', *Journal of Personality and Social Psychology*, 74: 1300–1309.

Cecchin, G., Lane, G. and Ray, W.A. (1994) *The Cybernetics of Prejudices in the Practice of Psychotherapy*, London: Karnac Books.

De Jong, P. and Berg, I.K. (2011) *Interviewing for Solutions*, 4th edn, Pacific Grove, CA: Brooks Cole Publishers. See also 2012 Instructor's Manual at: www.sfbta.org/trainingLinks.html (accessed 29 October 2014).

Deslauriers, L., Schelew, E. and Wieman, C. (2011) 'Improved learning in a large-enrollment physics class', *Science*, 332(6031): 862–64.

Dreyfus, H.L., Dreyfus, S.E. and Zadeh, L.A. (1987) 'Mind over machine: the power of human intuition and expertise in the era of the computer', *IEEE Expert*, 2: 110–11.

Epstein, E., Wiesner, M. and Duda, L. (2013) 'DSM and the diagnosis-MacGuffin: implications for the self and society', *Australian and New Zealand Journal of Family Therapy*, 34: 156–67.

Ericsson, K.A. (2006) 'The influence of experience and deliberate practice on the development of superior expert performance', in K.A. Ericsson, N. Charness, P.J. Feltovich and R.R. Hoffman (eds), *The Cambridge Handbook of Expertise and Expert Performance*, Cambridge: Cambridge University Press.

Flood, R.L. and Jackson, M.C. (1991) *Creative Problem Solving: Total Systems Intervention*, Chichester, UK: John Wiley & Sons.

Freire, P. (1982) 'Creating alternative research methods: learning to do it by doing it', in B. Hall, A. Gillette and R. Tandon (eds), *Creating Knowledge: A Monopoly* (pp. 29–37), New Delhi, India: Society for Participatory Research in Asia.

Furman, B. and Ahola, T. (1992) *Pickpockets on a Nudist Camp: The Systemic Revolution in Psychotherapy*, Dulwich, UK: Dulwich Centre Publications.

Gibbs, G. (1994) *Improving Student Learning*, Oxford: Oxford Centre for Staff Development.

Goolishian, H. (1990). 'Therapy as a linguistic system: hermeneutics, narrative and meaning', unpublished manuscript.

Greenhalgh, T., Howick, J. and Maskrey, N. (2014) 'Evidence based medicine: a movement in crisis', *BMJ*, 348: g3725.

Hermans, H.J.M. (2014) 'Self as a society of I-positions: a dialogical approach to counseling', *Journal of Humanistic Counselling*, 53: 134–59.

Hermans, H.J.M. and Gieser, T. (2011) *Handbook of Dialogical Self Theory*, Cambridge: Cambridge University Press.

Hermans, H.J.M. and Hermans-Jansen, E. (2003) 'Dialogical processes and development of the self', in J. Valsiner and K. Connolly (eds), *Handbook of Developmental Psychology* (pp. 534–59), New York: Sage.

Hermans, H.J.M., Kempen, H.J.G. and Van Loon, R.J.P. (1992) 'The dialogical self: beyond individualism and relationism', *American Psychologist*, 47: 23–33.

Ison, R. and Blackmore, C. (2014) 'Designing and developing a reflexive learning system for managing systemic change', *Systems*, 2: 119–36.

Kahneman, D. (2012) *Thinking, Fast and Slow*. London: Penguin.

Kogan, M. and Gale, J.E. (1997) 'Decentering therapy: textual analysis of a narrative therapy session', *Family Process*, 36: 101–26.

Kolb, D. (1983) *Experiential Learning: Experience as the Source of Learning and Development*, Englewood Cliffs, NJ: Prentice Hall.

Liddle, H., Breunlin, D. and Schwartz, R. (1988) *Handbook of Family Therapy Training and Supervision*, New York: Guilford.

McCaffrey, T. (2012) 'Innovation relies on the obscure: a key to overcoming the classic functional fixedness problem', *Psychological Science*, 23(3): 215–18.

Markus, H. and Nurius, P. (1986) 'Possible selves', *American Psychologist*, 41: 954–69.

Markus, H. and Wurf, E. (1987) 'The dynamic self-concept: a social psychological perspective', *Annual Review of Psychology*, 38: 299–337.

Martin, J. and Sugarman, J. (2001) 'Is the self a kind of understanding?', *Journal for the Theory of Social Behaviour*, 31: 103–14.

Maturana, H.R. (2002) 'Autopoiesis, structural coupling and cognition: a history of these and other notions in the biology of cognition', *Cybernetics and Human Knowing*, 9(3/4): 5–34.

Morgan, G. (1993) *Imaginization*, London: Sage.

Morgan, G. (1997) *Creative Organization Theory*, London: Sage.

Munton, A., Silvester, J., Stratton, P. and Hanks, H. (1999) *Attributions in Action*, Chichester, UK: John Wiley & Sons.

Pilling, S. and Roth, A. (2011) 'Competence frameworks for the delivery and supervision of psychological therapies', available at: www.ucl.ac.uk/clinical-psychology/CORE/competence_frameworks.htm (accessed 20 October 2014).

Rober, P. (2005) 'The therapist's self in dialogical family therapy: some ideas about not-knowing and the therapist's inner conversation', *Family Process*, 44: 479–97.

Rorty, R. (1989) *Contingency, Irony and Solidarity*, New York: Cambridge University Press.

Schön, D.A. (1990) *Educating the Reflective Practitioner: Towards a New Design for Teaching and Learning*, San Francisco, CA: Jossey-Bass.

Simon, G.M. (2006) 'The heart of the matter: a proposal for placing the self of the therapist at the center of family therapy research and training', *Family Process*, 45: 331–44.

Sio, U.N. and Ormerod, T.C. (2009) 'Does incubation enhance problem solving? A meta-analytic review', *Psychological Bulletin*, 135(1): 94–120.

Smith, J.D. (2014) 'Self-concept: autopoiesis as the basis for a conceptual framework', *Systems Research and Behavioral Science*, 31: 32–46.

Steiner, S., Stromwall, L.K., Brzuzy, S. and Gerdes, K. (1999) 'Using cooperative learning strategies in social work education', *Journal of Social Work Education*, 35: 253–64.

Stratton, P. (2003a) 'Causal attributions during therapy I: responsibility and blame', *Journal of Family Therapy*, 25: 134–58.

Stratton, P. (2003b) 'Causal attributions during therapy II: reconstituted families and parental blaming', *Journal of Family Therapy*, 25: 159–78.

Stratton, P. (2003c) 'Contemporary families as contexts for development: contributions from systemic family therapy', in J. Valsiner and K. Connolly (eds), *Handbook of Developmental Psychology* (pp. 333–57), New York: Sage.

Stratton, P. (2005) 'A model to coordinate understanding of active autonomous learning', *Journal of Family Therapy*, 27(3): 217–36.

Stratton, P. (2007) 'Dialogical construction of the selves of trainees as competent researchers', *Journal of Family Therapy*, 29: 342–5.

Stratton, P. (2013) 'Manuals: a secure base for playful therapy?', *Human Systems*, 24: 181–92.

Stratton, P.M., Heard, D.H., Hanks, H.G., Munton, A.G., Brewin, C.R. and Davidson, C. (1986) 'Coding causal beliefs in natural discourse', *British Journal of Social Psychology*, 25: 299–313.

Stratton, P., Preston-Shoot, M. and Hanks, H. (1990) *Family Therapy: Training and Practice*, Birmingham, UK: Venture Press.

Stratton, P., Hanks, H., Campbell, H. and Hatcher, S. (1993) 'Countertransference in systems thinking and practice', *Journal of Social Work Practice*, 7: 181–94.

Stratton, P., Reibstein, J., Lask, J., Singh, R. and Asen, E. (2011) 'Competences and occupational standards for systemic family and couples therapy', *Journal of Family Therapy*, 33: 123–43.

Sung-Chan, P.P.L. (2000) 'Putting Schön's reciprocal-reflection theory into practice', *Cybernetics and Human Knowing*, 7: 17–30.

Tajino, A. and Smith, C. (2005) 'Exploratory practice and soft systems methodology', *Language Teaching Research*, 9: 448–69.

Chapter 3

Mind the map

Circular processes between the therapist, the client and the therapist's personal life

Per Jensen

Introduction

A part of any PPD process should be both to reflect on what therapists learn and bring home from working as a therapist and on what they bring into therapy from their personal and private experiences. Psychotherapy process research emphasises the importance of the therapeutic relationship as both a starting point for a successful therapeutic process and as the medium for change (Høglend 1999; Wampold 2001; Norcross 2010). However, when it comes to the ways in which psychotherapists' personal and private experiences influence their clinical practice and their relationship with their clients, it is difficult to find relevant research. "While considerable research has examined how clients learn from psycho-therapists, there is only sparse literature on what therapists learn from their therapy clients" (Hatcher *et al.* 2012). The same seems to be the case when we look into psychotherapy research the other way around, on how working as a psychotherapist influences the therapist's personal and private life (Jensen 2008a; Lerøy 2008; Hatcher *et al.* 2012).

In clinical practice, the circular descriptions of processes between the therapist, the client and the therapist's personal life should be understood as ongoing, continuous and as an integrated part of clinical practice. Jim Sheehan's chapter in this book is an example of an integrative description of circular processes going both ways (Sheehan, Chapter 8, this volume). However, sometimes, it is relevant to study one way at a time, either from therapy to 'home' or from 'home' to therapy.

In this chapter, we discuss what therapists learn from their psychotherapy clients and how this affects their personal and professional lives, and what therapists bring into the therapy room from their own personal and private life experiences.

When it comes to what therapists bring into the therapy room, 'the map of relational resonance' offers an understanding of the different ways in which therapists' personal and private experiences create a context both for their therapeutic work and for the development and maintenance of therapeutic rela-tionships (Jensen 2008a). We will discuss some key findings from psychotherapy research concerning the relationship between the therapist and their clients, and provide a context for the presentation of the map of relational resonance. The map of relational resonance will be used in this chapter to widen relational understandings both for family therapy practice and for family therapy education. The map might have process implications for all counselling and psychotherapy practice.

Power and context

Psychotherapy in general and family therapy in particular may be viewed as practices of power and should, to some extent, be viewed as such. When it comes to topics such as gender (Burck and Daniel 1995), ethnic minority situations (Hildebrand 1998; Cross and Papadopoulos 2001) and professional culture (White and Epston 1990; Ekeland 2001), the need to analyse power relations seems to be as pressing today as it was earlier.

In constructing the map of relational resonance, I have used the concept of power to understand the influence on clients from the family therapist's personal and private values and culture. Foucault claims that power is relational and appears in all kinds of relationships. He further claims that power gains momentum as more people come to accept the particular views associated with a belief system as a form of common knowledge. Belief systems define their authority figures, such as priests in a church or medical doctors. Within such a belief system, ideas seem to deal with what is *right* and what is *wrong*, and similarly, with what is *normal* and what is *deviant* (Schaanning 1993). The concept of the psychotherapy relationship as a type of power relationship is not mentioned in many handbooks and textbooks in the psychotherapy field (Hougaard 2004; Lambert 2004; Duncan *et al.* 2010). In professional practice, the issue of power should be addressed, analysed and discussed.

Resonance

Mony Elkaïm introduces the concept of resonance to help us understand the dynamics of how one part of life may influence another. He says: "Resonance occurs when the same rule or feeling appears to be present in different but related systems" (Elkaïm 1997: xxvii). What occurs then is a kind of symmetry that invites the person to relate in certain or similar ways to what is going on. I will emphasise *resonance* as a concept for giving meaning to the circular processes that occur between the therapist, their clients, and the therapist's personal life.

Martha Rogers develops our understanding of resonance further by presenting it in a broader relational perspective. She says that resonance with the environment sometimes may be "harmonic, sometimes cacophonous, sometimes dissonant" (Rogers 1970: 219).

Relational resonance

The concept of resonance is developed to include both personal resonance and relational resonance. This means that resonance both takes place within a therapist's mind and emotions or in the individual family members' minds (personal resonance), and at the same time between the therapist and the family or client (relational resonance).

This concept of resonance is developed to include parallel connections (i.e. what occurs when a client or a family communicates and presents narratives that remind the therapist of his or her own personal and private experiences). The awareness is not only intellectual and sometimes possibly outside conscious awareness, but also comprises an embodied awareness. The aspects we are studying here are the resonances between a family therapist's personal and private life and his or her professional life. The emphasis on resonance will be developed to include several related concepts that add new meaning to the findings through "the map of relational resonance" (Jensen 2008a).

Resonance from therapeutic practice to the therapist's personal life

Resonances from professional practice to personal and private life are well known among many professionals. Architects' and designers' homes often reflect their professional taste and views. Psychotherapists' professional practice may also resonate into their personal and private life. Here, we will present three pieces of research on this area. These are Hatcher *et al.* (2012), Jensen (2008a) and Lerøy (2008). Some categories from Hatcher *et al.*'s research will be used to illustrate what therapists bring home.

In a qualitative, exploratory study by Hatcher *et al.* (2012), nine researchers interviewed 61 psychologists across North America in order to see what psychotherapists may have learned from their clients, and how their clients have affected them personally and professionally. Here, we are only going to report on the influence on their personal life.

In the research, the participants' elaborated responses were coded thematically and narrative data illustrate the most frequent themes. Informants responded to nine open-ended questions developed by a group of senior, practicing clinical psychologists on what they learned about: life lessons, relationships, ethical decision-making, coping, courage, wisdom, psychopathology, personality, cultural differences, and lifespan development. The therapists reported that they were learning a lot across each of the questions. Hatcher *et al.* (2012) quote two of the informants, and say:

> "We learn more from our clients as the years roll on and more from [each subsequent] client to pass on." In particular, therapists report learning lessons of patience, resiliency, non-judgmental listening, and respect for difference from the clients with whom they work. As one therapist said, "I used to believe that there could be one moment in therapy or one moment in life where things get solved . . . and then life becomes easy . . . I've come to understand that . . . conflicts are slowly resolved.
>
> (p. 5)

Therapists drew the line from their practice to their own life and, after having told how they think about therapy, they took it further in to their own lives by saying, "even when difficult things happen in my life" (Hatcher *et al.* 2012: 5). Here, we will look at how the topics of relationships, courage and coping resonate into the therapist's personal and private life.

Relationships

When Hatcher *et al.* asked therapists what they learned from their clients about relationships, 95 per cent indicated their own relationships were affected by their practice. One said, "I'm pretty much analyzing my own relationships all the time to keep a check on them" (Hatcher *et al.* 2012: 6). Not all only learned positive skills from their clients. One therapist said, "Being a therapist makes one really aware; sometimes it would be nice not to be so aware" (Hatcher *et al.* 2012: 6).

In my research (Jensen 2008a), similar resonances were reported (e.g. in a situation where one informant decided to separate from her husband of many years, still having two younger children). She worked in a family counselling office at that time, and she says:

> I got something of a flying start with my own divorce by having encountered many questions concerning second marriage and stepchildren and one's own children's relationship with stepfathers. That whole arena there, to have encountered that at work before I was there myself, gave me a bit of a flying start.
>
> (Jensen 2008a: 127)

This is one example of how a therapist might bring clinical experiences from the therapy room into his or her own personal and private life. In this case, it came to be a preparation to the therapist's own divorce process.

Courage

In Hatcher *et al.*'s study, the therapist's responses to the question about courage were often passionate "and admiring of clients' courage in the face of adversity, including the courage to engage in psychotherapy" (Hatcher *et al.* 2012: 9). The clinical work with clients sometimes put the therapists' difficulties in their own lives in perspective. One of the informants says:

> At times when I sort of think 'oh poor me,' I think of [my clients] and . . . I have nothing to really whine about . . . I feel if they can do it, I can do it. It serves to lift me up.
>
> (Hatcher *et al.* 2012: 9)

When summing up their findings about courage, Hatcher *et al.* (2012) claim, "Therapists almost uniformly report feeling hope from the courage they observe in their clients" (p. 9).

Coping

According to Hatcher *et al.* (2012), the main theme for coping seems to be "whatever works." Their research shows that therapists note that coping mechanisms often are influenced by the individual's values. One therapist says:

> I don't think we can give [coping skills] to people. I think we need to help them find it and establish a foothold and expand on it, but it has to come from some kind of internal structure rather than from an external knowledge base.
>
> (Hatcher *et al.* 2012: 8)

In my research (Jensen 2008a), informants report that friends from time to time want them to be an expert, and to tell them what to do in difficult situations. In one example, female friends ask my informant to explain men and male friends to explain women. He says that his contribution to questions such as this is to encourage the one asking to go home and learn to know their man or woman. He says that is better than reading tons of books about such topics. The informant also claims that it is more difficult to be a parent than to be a therapist. However, he hopes that his family has felt that he uses his time in conversations with them. "It has something to do with, how shall I put it, something to do with tuning in to each other," he says (Jensen 2008a: 128).

Lerøy (2008) has investigated experiences in living with a family therapist, interviewing three family therapists and three spouses/partners of a family therapist. The spouses/partners all agree that they have learned much about communication from their spouses'/partners' ways of communicating. Some of the spouses/partners use what they have learned in their own private life and professional work. One of them remarked:

> "I think there is a lot of communication here, which I have learnt from her. And I bring that with me." At work he would think about how to communicate matters, and says: "Well, I did think about how to say things, if the issues were challenging. How should I do this on a day-to-day basis? I thought like, how will he react if I say it like *this*. Compared to if I say it like that . . . At what time you bring it up can also be of importance . . . So these are things, which I have gotten from her."
>
> (Lerøy 2008: 60, emphasis in original)

As we see, it is not only therapists that might learn from working with clients, but sometimes also their spouses and partners. We will now explore the connections between the personal and private experiences and the therapists' clinical practice through presenting the map of resonance.

Mind the map: the map of relational resonance

The therapeutic relationship is one of the factors that promote change in psycho-therapy. How this element in the therapeutic process adds meaning to clinical practice is important to understand (Wampold 2001; Lambert 2004; Skovholt and Jennings 2004; Orlinsky and Rønnestad 2005). From this perspective, the influence of the therapist's personal and private experience on the therapeutic process is one important factor to take into account and understand. Sullivan, Skovholt and Jennings' claim in their research that master therapists describe their awareness of their "selves" as "an agent of change in the relationship" (Sullivan *et al.* 2005: 58). When Elkaïm (1997) mentions "the same rule or feeling" talking about resonance, it is possible to think that rules are articulated or possible to articulate and that feelings are unarticulated and can be brought into conscious awareness or as a part of analogue communication. Feelings may of course be articulated, but the articulation is not the feeling, in the same way that the map is not the territory.

The map of relational resonance was derived from grounded theory research (Jensen 2008a) and offers us a language for analysing psychotherapeutic processes. It also carries potential as an evaluation tool both in family therapy education and in evaluating clinical practice in general, and is meant to be an aid to supervision and training. The concepts that are developed in this chapter are based on an understanding of the possible interactions between the therapist and the family or client as different types of *relational resonance*. We are looking for influences

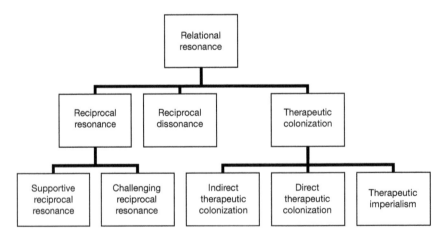

Figure 3.1 The map of relational resonances
Source: Jensen (2012); reprinted with permission

from the personal and private to the professional life. The map of resonance is meant to promote further reflections on the understanding of what is going on *in the therapy room* when it comes to how the interactional processes are influenced by the therapists' personal and private experiences. An overview of the structure and the concepts used in the map of relational resonance is presented below:

This relational map of resonances was developed from my grounded theory research project to explore and explain how systemic family therapists influence clients within the framework of their own personal and private backgrounds (Jensen 2008a). We will now take a closer look at the different categories in the map.

Reciprocal resonance

Reciprocal resonance covers therapeutic meetings where the client's history or situation recalls memories and emotions for the therapists that connect the therapist and the clients in a common way. This connection might be fully articulated, partly articulated or unarticulated.

Reciprocal resonance is described as the relationship between the family therapist's life experiences and his or her clients' living through similar life events. These stories vary, from the therapists who find ways to handle and learn from these experiences, to those who find themselves in a personal crisis that makes it impossible to go on working as a family therapist in that situation.

Reciprocal resonance covers a therapeutic process where the relationship between the therapist and their clients has the character of mutual understanding. "Indeed, of the multitude of factors that account for success in psychotherapy, clinicians of different orientations converge on this point: The therapeutic relationship is the cornerstone" (Norcross 2010: 114).

Reciprocal resonances may be punctuated as more or less supportive and more or less challenging both by therapists and clients. One main finding in my research project is that six of the seven therapist participant informants could tell important stories of how their personal and private experiences in life have influenced their therapeutic practice. The one informant who did not tell stories that linked his personal and private life to his therapeutic practice was open to look for such links and considered such links to be logical and possible.

Supportive reciprocal resonance

Supportive reciprocal resonance may be viewed as the secure base of therapy (Dallos and Vetere 2009) and as part of joining in family therapy (Minuchin 1977; Jensen 2008a). However, supportive reciprocal resonance is meant to cover a more specific and narrow part of a therapy session or a therapeutic encounter. Supportive reciprocal resonance describes the elements in joining that stem from the therapist's personal and private life and that are brought into the therapy by the therapist's interaction with clients. Supportive reciprocal resonance forms the frame for a sequence or sequences in therapy, in which resonance from the client's stories, manners, behaviours, culture and background add meaning to or support the therapist's understanding in a way that comes to affect the relationship between the therapist and the client(s) and might give the therapy a new direction based on this supportive resonance.

Karen had the experience growing up that nobody listened to her. When she came to therapy, she was listened to for the first time. When she later became a therapist herself, listening to everybody became her credo. Karen's interest in talking to and listening to each member of the family in the therapy room may be seen as an important kind of supportive reciprocal resonance that forms the starting point for any therapy session (Jensen 2008a).

All informants claim that their personal and private experience has been meaningful and supportive in their therapeutic practice. In a general way, the interest in talking and listening to people may be seen as an important kind of supportive reciprocal resonance. Perhaps this is the most basic starting point of them all for a systemic family therapist. If so, this should have implications for training.

Challenging reciprocal resonance

Challenging reciprocal resonance forms the frame for a sequence or sequences in therapy, where the resonance from the client's stories, manners, behaviours or culture and background challenge the therapist in a way that comes to affect the relationship between the therapist and the client(s) and gives the therapy a new direction based on this challenging resonance. This may limit or endanger the therapeutic relationship, but it may also offer some new directions and possibilities for the therapeutic process.

One of the informant's stories is an example of challenging reciprocal resonance. Challenging reciprocal resonance occurred when she met with a woman frustrated because of her sick husband. The woman was healthy and would be living with this sick man for a long time. This story gave resonance to some of the therapist's experiences with her own sick and dying husband. She said that she recognised aspects of her own experience in the woman's stories. She thought it was a mistake for her to go on without commenting on her own parallel situation. She said to this client: "I have been through similar things in my life. And it affects me and it makes it so that I think that you should go to another therapist" (Jensen 2008a: 143). The woman chose to go to another therapist and my informant had to take sick leave not long after this.

Another example of challenging reciprocal resonance is another informant's link between her experiences as a young woman in a religious charismatic group and her view of these groups today. She says that she is one of the few "that dare to say that I wish that (the charismatic group) would be taken away from patients" (Jensen 2008a: 109). She does not refer to any professional explanations or research to give reasons for her opinion, but to her own personal experience with being a member of such a group.

However, in general, I suggest that it is very dangerous and unethical to use one's own personal experience as the *only* reason for this kind of advice. This could lead to what I call 'therapeutic colonialism' or 'therapeutic imperialism'.

Reciprocal dissonance

Cognitive dissonance is a concept from social psychology. Saugstad (2007) refers to Festinger (1957), who points out that cognitive dissonance represents lack of accord between values, attitudes, ideas, understandings and experiences in a person's life. In our lives, we strive for dissonance reduction.

Reciprocal dissonance occurs when clients awaken feelings and behaviour in the therapist that he or she finds unpleasant and that hinder his or her curiosity and empathy and drive the therapist to reduce or end the therapeutic relationship. Some clients act and behave in a manner that some therapists find hard to manage. Two typical topics that trigger some therapists emotionally are clients that tell the same story over and over again or repeat the same theme over and over again. Another topic is complaining, including those clients who complain without appearing to make any move to change. If the therapy ends because of such topics, both the therapist and the client(s) will probably end up in an unfruitful therapeutic process. Cases such as this should be brought to supervision and/or the client(s) should, if possible, get a new therapist.

Therapeutic colonisation

Therapeutic colonisation is one special form of resonance. Colonisation is best known as a political concept used as a framework to understand what goes on between powerful nations and their relations with developing countries. Jürgen Habermas built on the ideas of Talcott Parsons in his use of the term 'colonisation' when he speaks about "colonization of the life world" (Schaanning 1993). Lifeworld is what Habermas (1987) calls "the 'background' environment of competences, practices, and attitudes representable in terms of one's cognitive horizon." In linguistics, the concepts 'linguistic colonisation' and 'linguistic imperialism' were coined to develop an understanding of how language constructs and constrains our world view (Vedeler 2007).

When I use the concept *therapeutic colonisation*, it is to describe how a systemic family therapist's personal culture, experience and moral values in different ways influence his or her therapeutic practice. Therapeutic colonisation represents the creation of a context that reduces the sphere in which reciprocal communication operates. The reduced sphere for reciprocal communication is based on the therapist's use of his or her power to, for example, define and introduce topics for conversation.

Indirect therapeutic colonisation

Indirect therapeutic colonisation occurs when the therapist's own personal and private experience influences systemic family therapy in an unplanned and unarticulated way. The therapist is not always aware of what is going on, and this may create a context that could be understood to be different from what the therapist considers as his or her professional practice. The specifics of their power relationship might be hidden both for the therapist and the client.

One therapist who claimed that he never used his private experiences in therapeutic processes realised, after analysing a therapy session, that his personal ideals of going back home to tell about his life situation influenced one specific therapy session profoundly (Jensen 2008b). In my interview with him, he emphasised why he avoided giving advice, so I was surprised when, in a video from a therapy session, he asked the couple if they had talked about their marital problems with anyone, and what they felt about telling their parents. He then said the following to the couple: "One could of course say to parents and acquaintances, to family and friends that one is going to family counselling, so that they will understand that this isn't something one has done with a light heart, for example" (Jensen 2008a: 155).

At first, I did not understand his reasoning for giving this near-advice to the couple. But then I remembered from his first interview with me, one of his own private stories from his time as a young student. His girlfriend became pregnant and he decided not to marry her. She would keep the child and he would become a father, his father and mother would be grandparents and his siblings would be uncles and aunts. He knew he had to go home to his pietistic parents and the rest of the family and explain that there would be a new member of the family and that he would not marry the child's mother. In the late 1960s, this was a difficult message to give in a Christian, pietistic environment in eastern Norway. They 'had to' include a new member in the family born outside marriage, a happening viewed as terrible in many families. However, his family included the child as one of their own. They managed to be real grandparents to the child. In his home, "it was possible to have an open dialogue about most topics," he says.

In my second research interview with him, I decided to link this good experience from his private life to his intervention when he had "advised" the couple to go home and tell their parents. When I met him, I was prepared for him to reject this interpretation or to ignore it, or even that he might be angry with me for trying to suggest he acted against his own professional principals. I presented my idea about this connection for him and said:

> You said that you thought it might have been an idea for them to tell their family and maybe their friends. And then I thought that that was something you also did when something dramatic happened to you and in your family. The first thing you did was to go home to your mother and father . . . to say that there is actually a grandchild on the way.
>
> (Jensen 2008a: 156)

When he heard this, he was stunned and obviously moved, with tears in his eyes, and he remarked, "I can feel that I'm moved." When I pointed out to him that he was close to advising the couple to tell their parents and siblings about their problems, he confirmed that to him, these kinds of stories represent an important part of his value base in his understanding of being a family. At the same time, he was surprised that he really said what he said or gave that advice. To do this was contrary to his ideas about how therapy should be done.

Direct therapeutic colonisation

When direct therapeutic colonisation occurs, it is the therapist that uses his or her power to define the topics for discussion despite what the clients ask for or introduce as their concerns or needs. In this way, the sphere in which reciprocal communication operates is reduced, and a power relationship is thus developed. Direct therapeutic colonisation is often articulated as, and may take the form of, clinical methods.

One informant showed one example of therapeutic colonisation in the video of a first therapy session. The couple she met made a relatively clear and distinct request for help. The woman opened by saying that they had decided to divorce, but as they have two children they needed help to communicate. The therapist asked about the family as a whole and all their severe problems; the husband's alcohol abuse was only one among all these problems. However, after these opening questions and answers, the therapist used almost the whole session to ask and talk about the husband's alcohol abuse (Jensen 2008a).

When I came back to my informant for the next research interview, she related this to the fact that she thinks her own husband drinks too much, and said, "It isn't more than one or two years ago that I sat in a Family Consultation Office and said 'I'm leaving if this doesn't get sorted out.'" (Jensen 2008a: 204). Although she was aware of this parallel when she conducted the session, she did not manage to come out of it or give the therapy session the direction the couple asked for. Her repeated punctuation of the husband's alcohol abuse reduced her ability to listen to their needs and what they came for.

Therapeutic imperialism

The concept of imperialism is a political one coined in the late 1500s to reflect and give a name to the politics of expansion from Europe into Africa and America. The concept is integral to different political theories and is used to give an understanding of how power may be used to oppress a state, culture or a people. Imperialism is usually defined as a term applied to a state that tries by force to conquer and shape other societies to conformity with its own ideas or values. In addition, if we look at the concept from an etymological point of view, we find that 'imperial' stands for 'order' or 'command'. Therefore, the concept is most appropriate in describing a relationship where the distribution of power is unevenly divided and where one part uses power to support his or her concerns.

I will define 'therapeutic imperialism' as a situation or a sequence in therapy where the therapists *using direct power* articulate a personal value base or personal experiences from their private life that forms the direct background for clinical interventions, against the will of one or more members of the family in therapy. The use of power and going *against the clients' explicit will* makes the difference between therapeutic colonialism and therapeutic imperialism.

I have also coined the concept 'therapeutic imperialism' to create a framework for understanding the action one informant took in the family where the father refused to let his new children know that he had two children from a former marriage. Based on her own experience from a parallel connection as a child, she stated that it was wrong to keep this kind of secret from children, and against the father's will she told his new children that they had two half-siblings. However, I question seriously whether personal and private experiences and values on their own are a sufficient foundation for clinical interventions such as this.

This example illustrates how a personal and private situation may form and organise a therapy session so that 'therapeutic imperialism' can take place. This illustrates how a therapist may lose his or her curiosity and openness and let his or her own private situation govern the therapy session. However, once these processes are articulated, they are open for supervision, self-reflection and adaptation. 'Indirect therapeutic colonisation', on the other hand, is often unavailable or difficult to discover unless observation is a part of the way of working.

These examples above have shown that different kinds of 'therapeutic colonisation' may occur even in the practice of a very experienced therapist. When in a sequence the highest context seems to be the therapist's personal and private value base, a sequence of the therapy session may be formatted by these values. These examples may give a rationale for regular direct supervision, not only as part of family therapy training programmes, but also for qualified therapists.

Discussion

The use of the therapist's power to form and frame the conversation makes it necessary to bring in discussions of ethical accountability into the understanding of systemic family therapy. At the same time, theory can be a basis for being held accountable for our ideas, and supervision and personal therapy help us to identify and understand our prejudices.

Olkowska (2013) did some research on how therapists used their own experiences actively in therapeutic processes. Findings from Olkowska's research show how family therapists use self-disclosure in family therapy practice when they work with families with children and adolescents. Some of her informants say they prefer to use examples from their own lives rather than from a book, and another one said that you know you have got a 'customer' when the client asks for your own experiences.

Therapeutic ideas are deeply embedded in our culture and society. We are all subject to similar social discourses, and therapeutic ideas are a part of a culture and come forward in a culture. For example, the idea of the 'self' is much weaker and of another kind in some Eastern cultures. In his book *Rewriting the Self: History, Memory, Narrative*, Mark Freeman claims that "a life history, rather than being a 'natural' way of accounting for self, is one that is thoroughly enmeshed within a specific and unique form of discourse and understanding" (Freeman 1993: 28, cited in Johansson 2005: 230). Personal stories such as biography or personal narratives are nothing natural or universal, but are culturally constructed.

Diverse social constructions of the self, faith and religion, and other cultural differences are among the issues that make it necessary to develop the map of resonance as a tool in family therapy education and supervision. When we need to reflect upon the links between private life and professional practice, should we be asking for therapy, consultation or supervision (Jones 2003)? This is often supported by the idea of a strict division between what is private and what is professional. Today, this division between professional and private seems to confuse our understanding of psychotherapy. A more fruitful position could be to look for how to achieve an appropriate balance between the 'private' and the 'professional' (Hurst 2001; Protinsky and Coward 2001; Graff *et al.* 2003; Roberts 2005).

In the research of Hatcher *et al.* (2012), the participants showed what and how they responded to topics introduced to them by their clients. The therapists reported that they were learning a lot across each of these themes.

In my research, the therapists' own ideas about what governs their therapeutic practice were often a main source of understanding what was going on in a therapy session. These professional ideas may, however, from time to time, be overruled by other aspects than those considered to belong to professional practice. When a therapist claims that he or she is governed by his or her professional background and experience, he or she is claiming that theory, research, ethical and other professional considerations form the *context* for his or her therapeutic work.

Most of the informants in my research project have been in personal therapy themselves to help with their own life problems. Some of them directly refer to these experiences as very important steps in their own development as family therapists. When Orlinsky and Rønnestad (2005) carried out their comprehensive research on how psychotherapists develop, 3 in 10 of the Western therapists actually were in personal therapy when they participated in the study. They also found that:

> Clinicians with no experience of personal therapy showed the lowest rate of felt progress and the highest rates of regress and stasis. By contrast, practitioners who were currently in therapy showed the highest rate of progress and the lowest rate of stasis.
>
> (Orlinsky and Rønnestad 2005: 121)

The question is whether, in addition to PPD work, the time is right to reintroduce discussion and reflection over the need for and benefits of having personal therapy as a compulsory part of the education programme for a student who wants to qualify as a family therapist.

The map of resonance could also be discussed from an ethical point of view. Some of the categories in the map are closer to ethical considerations than others. One example of a finding that needs ethical consideration is the informant's story about the relationship between her own personal and private values and experiences with a half-brother and her encounter with a family in a parallel situation. That she forced her own values on the family could have resulted in a violation of the father's ideals and way of organising his own family life. According to her, this was not what happened. However, stories such as this bring up the need for discussing family therapy practice in an ethical framework and the continuing need for ethical guidelines.

In the creation of ethical accountability, ethical considerations are important when reports about different types of therapeutic colonialism are received from therapeutic practice. Family therapists are meant to respect and support clients' own values and culture as a point of departure for therapy. The therapists need to carefully take up and discuss it when ethical standards collide or conflict inside a family or between the family and therapists. In these situations, applications of the therapists' power are obvious and kept as visible as possible for all involved (e.g. in child protection work).

Conclusions

This chapter has shown how a therapist's clinical practice might influence and stimulate the therapist's personal and private life and even his or her partners. The other way around, the therapist's personal and private experiences from their own life might sometimes be understood as a part of the clinical practice. When working with PPD processes, we should be reflecting on both what therapists learn and bring home from working as a therapist and on what we bring into therapy from our personal and private experiences in our own lives. This is necessary if we aim to get a wide understanding of what is going on in the therapy room.

In clinical practice, the circular descriptions of processes between the therapist and the client, and the therapist's personal life should be understood as ongoing, continuum and as an integrated part of clinical practice. Jim Sheehan's chapter in this book shows that therapy also could be understood as an integrative description of circular processes going both ways (Sheehan, Chapter 8, this volume). The research in this chapter shows that both what therapists bring 'home' and what they bring from 'home' to the therapy room is relevant knowledge to work on in PPD processes.

Exercise: Connections between personal and professional narratives

The aim of this exercise is to investigate, reflect on and discover links and patterns that connect personal and private narratives to professional practice.

The therapeutic self-group

A, B, C, D and E (the group might have 5–8 members)

E takes responsibility for keeping track of exact timing

Table 3.1 Steps

1	A	Tell a story about an experience from before the age of 12. Any story, but it must be about you.	5 minutes
	A	Tell a story about an experience from contemporary professional life. It is about you in practice.	5 minutes
	A	Turn back to the group and take notes during the group's reflection.	
2	B, C, D, E	Reflect and discuss the relationship between the two stories. The discussion is supposed to be a creative process based on the *available* information.	10 minutes
3	A, B, C, D, E	Include A in the conversation and A will get the possibility to comment on the reflections in step 2.	10 minutes

This exercise could be done several times. If the first narrative for one member of the group (A) is from before 12 years of age, the same person can tell a story from youth, next as an adult and so on. When a group goes on like this, the members are given possibilities to develop understanding of patterns that link their own personal and private experiences to their professional practices.

References

Burck, C. and Daniel, G. (1995) *Gender and Family Therapy*, London: Karnac.

Cross, M. and Papadopoulos, L. (2001) *Becoming a Therapist*, Hove, UK: Brunner-Routledge.

Dallos, R. and Vetere, A. (2009) *Systemic Therapy and Attachment Narratives: Applications in a Range of Settings*, London: Routledge.

Duncan, B., Miller, S.D., Wampold, B.E. and Hubble, M.A. (eds) (2010) *The Heart and Soul of Change: What Works in Therapy*, Washington, DC: American Psychological Association.

Ekeland, T.J. (2001) 'Den biomedisinske arkitekturen som maktdiskurs', *Fokus på familien*, 4, Oslo, Norway: Scandinavian University Press.

Elkaïm, M. (1997) *If You Love Me, Don't Love Me*, London: Jason Aronson.

Graff, J., Lund-Jacobson, D. and Wermer, A. (2003) 'X-files: the power of personal stories in private-professional consultation', *Human Systems*, 14: 17–32.

Habermas, J. (1987) *The Theory of Communicative Action*, Boston, MA: Beacon Press.

Hatcher, S., Kipper-Smith, A., Waddell, M., Uhe, M., West, J.S., Boothe, J.H., Frye, J.M., Tighe, K., Usselman, K.L. and Gingras, P. (2012) 'What therapists learn from psychotherapy clients: effects on personal and professional lives', *The Qualitative Report*, 17(95): 1–21.

Hildebrand, J. (1998) *Bridging the Gap: A Training Module in Personal and Professional Development*, London: Karnac.

Høglend, P. (1999) 'Psychotherapy research: new findings and implications for training and practice', *The Journal of Psychotherapy Practice and Research*, 8: 257–63.

Hougaard, E. (2004) *Psykoterapi: teori og forskning*, København, Denmark: Dansk psykologisk forlag.

Hurst, A. (2001) *Master's Degree Dissertation Critique*, London: Tavistock Clinic and East London University.

Jensen, P. (2008a) *The Narratives Which Connect: A Qualitative Research Approach to the Narratives Which Connect Therapists' Personal and Private Lives to Their Family Therapy Practices*, Doctorate of Systemic Psychotherapy awarded by the University of East London in conjunction with the Tavistock Clinic, UK.

Jensen, P. (2008b) 'How to understand the lack of research that includes the meaning of therapist personal and private life in psychotherapy', *Human Systems*, 18(1–3): 190–211.

Jensen, P. (2012) 'Family therapy, personal life and therapeutic practice: the map of relational resonance as a language for analyzing psychotherapeutic processes', *Human Systems*, 23: 119–38.

Johansson, A. (2005) *Narrativ teori och metod*, Lund, Sweden: Studentlitteratur.

Jones, E. (2003) 'Working with the "self" of the therapist in consultation', *Human Systems*, 14(1): 7–16.

Lambert, M.J. (2004) *Handbook of Psychotherapy and Behavior Change*, New York: John Wiley & Sons.

Lerøy, A.M. (2008) *Mellom liv og lære kan det vere kort veg*, master's thesis, Diakonhjemmet University College, Norway.

Minuchin, S. (1977) *Familjer i terapi*, Stockholm, Sweden: Wahlström & Widestrand.

Norcross, J.C. (2010) 'The therapeutic relationship', in B.L. Duncan, S.D. Miller, B.E. Wampold and M.A. Hubble (eds), *The Heart and Soul of Change: Delivering What Works in Therapy* (2nd edn) (pp. 113–41), Washington, DC: American Psychological Association.

Olkowska, A. (2013) 'Fortsettelsen av jakten på etter X-files', *Fokus på familien*, 2, Oslo, Norway: Scandinavian University Press (pp. 117–33).

Orlinsky, D. and Rønnestad, M.H. (2005) *How Psychotherapists Develop*, Washington, DC: American Psychological Association.

Protinsky, H. and Coward, L. (2001) 'Developmental lessons of seasoned marital and family therapists: a qualitative investigation', *Journal of Marital and Family Therapy*, 27(3): 375–84.

Roberts, J. (2005) 'Transparency and self-disclosure in family therapy: dangers and possibilities', *Family Process*, 44(1): 45–63.

Rogers, M. (1970) *An Introduction to the Theoretical Basis of Nursing*, Philadelphia, PA: F.A. Davis Company.

Saugstad, P. (2007) *Psykologiens historie: en innføring i moderne psykologi*, Oslo, Norway: Gyldendal Akademisk.

Schaanning, E. (1993) 'Michel Foucault', in *Vestens tenkere*, Oslo, Norway: H. Aschehoug & Co.

Skovholt, T.M. and Jennings, L. (2004) *Master Therapists: Exploring Expertise in Therapy and Counseling*, Boston, MA: Pearson.

Sullivan, M.F., Skovholt, T.M. and Jennings, L. (2005) 'Master therapists' construction of the therapy relationship', *Journal of Mental Health Counseling*, 27(1): 48–70.

Vedeler, A.H. (2007) 'Den bekymrede vandringsmannen: John Shotter om Tom Andersen i samtale med Anne Hedvig Vedeler', *Fokus på familien*, 3, Oslo, Norway: Scandinavian University Press (pp. 166–77).

Wampold, B.E. (2001) *The Great Psychotherapy Debate*, London: Lawrence Erlbaum Associates.

White, M. and Epston, D. (1990) *Narrative Means to Therapeutic Ends*, London: W.W. Norton & Company.

Chapter 4

Supervision

Present within movements

Anne Hedvig Helmer Vedeler

In his book *The Shadow of the Sun*, Ryszard Kapuscinski (1998), a Polish journalist who lived for several decades on the African continent, notes how different cultures relate to disagreement and quarrels. Under the enormous mango tree in the village of Adofo, in the Ethiopian province of Wollega, the people gather for conferences:

> If someone in the village is quarreling with someone else, then the court convened beneath the tree will not try to ascertain the truth, or where justice lies, but will set itself the sole task of ending the conflict and conciliating the warring sides, while granting to each that he is in the right.

(p. 315)

Aims and ideas

In my opinion, programs for enhancing personal development for professionals of systemic practice should encourage an ongoing benevolent curiosity about themselves as persons in relation to others. I have during the last years explored how dialogical practices (Vedeler 2011; Anderson 2012; Seikkula and Arnkild 2013) might be a way of interacting with supervisees to produce greater awareness, both on my part and on theirs. In these groups, I have found how small details can make a big difference in our learning. Supervisees have reported that awareness of the here and now interactive moments that appear in supervision may have a spillover effect into other contexts, such as therapy and other domains of life.

This chapter will address the significance of being *present within movements*. Through an example, I will describe how a supervisor might compose (Shotter 2011) herself in the supervision group, taking in each 'situation' as novel, with potential for something new to be created. This requires that the supervisor is attentive to the vaguely sensed movements but not-yet-worded *feelings* expressed in the room. This attentive position involves feeling one's way into the 'world of the other' and listening to the uniqueness in what is expressed. The intention is to offer each supervisee ample space to tentatively explore what emerges by feeling their way in both their inner and outer relational evolving landscape. I call this *perpetual groping for meaning*[1] (i.e. how meaning emerges on the threshold between voices *in* and *in between* people through never-ending dialogues). It is a reminder of what the Russian philosopher Mikhail Bakhtin (1981) termed *heteroglossia* (i.e. how there is potential for an *indefinite* 'amount' of meaning immanent in every word we use, as well as in all experiences and situations). This way of talking means to be *tentative in our understanding* (Anderson 1997), *compassionate in our listening* (Lipari 2009) and allowing for *felt sense* (Gendlin 2003) to emerge. This entails a supervisor to engender a context that might feel safe enough to explore ambiguity, uncertainty, ambivalence, ruptures, discourses, hopes and dreams. Such openness is facilitated by listeners who are able to follow the one who talks, through a landscape that is not fixed. The supervisor's stance should elicit a pace where there is ample time to talk and to listen, to each other as well as to oneself.

This way of being *with* people is hard to describe. I hope the present tale can offer some clarity how groups of people *move in relation to each other* and how this may create profound transformations in the members' relationships in the group and in other domains of their lives.

Usually, I start by inviting the participants into a dialogue about what supervision can be and their expectations of it. Then the process is shaped by inviting each supervisee in turn to talk with me while the others are listening. We call this process *rounds*. These rounds may take half an hour or two days. It depends on the process and how much time we have.[2]

A tale: under the mango tree

The following is partly transcriptions and texts from a supervision group (inserted) and partly my comments and reflections about the events.

Outside my apartment door:

Six women had approached me through email and asked if I could be their supervisor during their last year of training. They were second year students of family therapy and systemic practice in a two-year program. That was about all I knew about them.

As I was preparing for this new group, making coffee, watering my plants and arranging some more chairs around the table, I was trying to memorise their names: *Karen, Ida, Marion, Lisa, Ellen* and *Susanne*.

The bell rang and when I opened the front door I was greeted by a small crowd of smiling middle-aged women, standing on the steps outside my apartment. They had all arrived at the same time, and were now filling my small hallway with their bodies, enthusiastic talk and laughter.

Well seated, coffee poured and some small talk, we started to talk about the group. The women told me that they had had 40 hours with their former supervisor.[3] "This is a very nice group, and we enjoy each other's company," was what I heard.

I proposed that we could take a round, share experiences and expectations. "Let's move on, but we're not in a hurry. I would like us to use time to get to know each other, and maybe get a sense of this group's culture and see how it develops."

Karen started by telling me about herself, where she worked and so on. I asked her how she had perceived supervision in other contexts and what she hoped for now. Karen said something about being open and curious, and that she had been very satisfied with the former supervisor. I wanted to hear some more concerning this satisfaction and Karen mentioned how she had been feeling *safe*. I wondered about the feeling of safety and Karen emphasised that it was *her* feeling, and that there might be different feelings in the group. I didn't follow up her remark, but made a mental note that "*something* is going on in this group."

Musicality

It was this *sense of something* I brought with me, much like what Daniel Stern (2010) would term musical contours, saturated with meaning but without words. As Wittgenstein (1953: 527) suggests: "Understanding a sentence is much more akin to understanding a theme in music than one might think." Bjørkvold (2005) asserts that sound, movement and rhythm are the *musical characteristics* of the human being. It is through these elements that people are coupled to each other. This is in correspondence with Malloch and Trevarthen (2009), who perceive dialogical musicality as a human capacity.

These ideas encouraged me to welcoming *improvisation* and attention to the keynotes of all present. Friis and Larsen (2006) are referring to improvisation as accepting the offer made by the other and allowing yourself to be changed. Daniel Stern (2010) compares dialogue with 'jam-sessions'. He points out that to play jazz, one must learn to get differences to function together, even though they are absolute contrasts. This requires that one modulates reciprocally with other musicians and the dynamic becomes a unique shared construction, in the same way as in dialogue.

I turned towards Ida. She too shared her expectations and how much she had enjoyed the group. Ida felt she could trust people and that she had been learning so much from everybody. "But," she hesitated, and there was a long gap of vibrating silence. "But?" I asked with a soft tone of voice, and a small smile. "Is there more, in that but?"

I am quite attentive towards how I 'appear' in situations such as this. I don't want to be perceived as demanding, just inviting. This means that I try to express a benevolent interest and at the same time giving my partner permission to turn down my invitation.

"But, eh, I don't really know since I wasn't in the middle of it," Ida's eyes swept around to the others. "I don't know if the rest . . ." she stopped again, and stared. "This sounds as if it's something we could talk about," I suggested tentatively. I didn't understand what it was, but I sensed that at least some of the nodding bodies were heavily burdened with this "something."

Lisa and Marion started to talk, filling in for each other. I understood that there had been some disagreement last time they were together, and something Ellen had said had hurt them. Ellen was silent, but then she burst out: "It was absolutely awful. I haven't slept well in these last weeks. I felt so miserable. I should have kept my mouth shut. Oh, why do I always act without thinking?" As they went on, I got the impression that Ellen had felt offended by *something* someone had said, and had expressed *something* that Marion and Lisa had felt was hurtful. It had happened just as they were about to finish the last supervision session, and they hadn't had the chance to talk about it. Ellen hadn't been talking to anyone. "Not even to your husband," Lisa seemed surprised. "No!" Marion and Lisa told that they had had some contact and talked about what had happened. Karen, Ida and Susanne all expressed a kind of bewilderment, they had felt the apprehension back then, but hadn't understood the implication it had had for the three others.

"Let's talk about this," I offered, feeling a kind of relief and a bit of excitement, having sensed this strain in the group and managed to participate in bringing it out into the open.

Bodily feeling

At this point, I felt softly spreading waves between my shoulder blades, then a tickling sensation in my chest, small movements in my stomach, down towards my tights and back again. I could feel how my body moved in the chair, first leaning forwards, and then settling backwards as if grounding myself in the situation. Without cognitively noticing it, I found myself having jumped into something unexpected and I *sensed* a demand for improvisation.

My response called for *answerability* (Bakhtin 1990), acting into the uniqueness of this particular event that required keen presence. This attentive position involves an approach to language as not decoding signs, but feeling one's way into the 'world of the other' and listening to the uniqueness in what is expressed. This *presence* means meeting every new situation with openness like blushing pre-juvenile innocence and still with utmost sincerity. It is about listening without creating order or coherence, without evaluation, judgment or assessment, but with an openness to be touched and transformed by the other. To be able to do this, I feel like I need to 'breathe the other in' the same way I take a newborn baby in and let it move me – there is nothing there to assess; it is just love.

There was a real sense of tension in the room. This *something* had hit hard and threatened to crack this group of women into pieces. I will not propose that I was happy or content with the situation; there was too much agony for that. Still, I *knew* that if we managed to find a way to go on, much could happen. I even felt that it could give the group a chance to experience how problems can be dissolved through dialogue. I suggested that I could talk with Lisa, Marion and Ellen, one at a time, and asked the three others if they could form a reflecting team (Andersen 1987). They all accepted the invitation. But first I suggested we should take a long break.

Ida stopped on her way out and asked:

"Are you anxious?"

"About what?" I replied.

"No, I don't know. But there are so much, eh, feelings here, so much hurt. Are you not afraid that you'll step on someone's toes?" Ida's eyes were full of concern.

"No, I think this is exciting and even stimulating in a way," I responded.

I don't know if I was completely honest, because I could feel a sort of insistent anticipation. Did I feel a kind of uncertainty? Could I manage this? Could I in the end make things worse? I had heard voices filled with despair and witnessed eyes full of anguish, and I wanted to be of help. Still, I didn't feel the need to contemplate this; instead, I prepared for being present with whatever turned up.

Tom Andersen (1987) advised us in situations such as this to 'not think, just look'. To me, this means to open my senses towards the coming, and not dwell on my thinking about what is to be said, or what has been said.

I had no other plan than initiating *a format* that could create an opportunity for talking and being listened to and experience being met, granting to each one that she *is in the right*.

> After having arranged ourselves in the room, I asked the reflecting team to listen with their 'appreciative ears' and with their 'hearts', explaining that what I meant was for them to "listen for the relationship the one who talks has to what she is talking about. You can hear that if you listen to the tone of voice, the gaps, the distinction, the pace and the words. When you respond, speak from the resonance it has created in your own body."

I was not going after *the* story. It was *the effect* on each one of those involved that needed to be welcomed. If we had pursued the content of the story, and tried to sort out *who* had said *what* to *whom* about *what*, I am certain we could have come into misunderstanding, blame and guilt. The negotiated cause of the event could become more important than the feelings that succeeded the happening.

The excessive trust in sorting things out, in order to create a story of an event, is not only an overestimated exercise; it is also a tricky business. "Life as it is lived is not story-like ... Lives include all sorts of extraneous details leading nowhere, but good stories do not" (Morson 1994: 19–20). The narratives function as a major intellectual device for *organising* into an intelligible whole what otherwise appears to be a collection of disconnected fragmentary events. This organisation of complex events has the possibility to create a shared meaning but just as well a potential for *circumscribing* the event as it is experienced.

I am sure we could have found stories about this event, stories that would have had causes and effects, but I am not sure it would have made it easier for the women to go on together. To sort out a problem as if it is a rational construction is what Wittgenstein (1953) calls *difficulties of the intellect*. Difficulty of *orientation* is different, and requires another way of relating. To relate to these kinds of difficulties, we need to explore many different relationships and stay open towards an indefinite 'amount' of meaning. A way of doing this is to keep on encouraging curiosity, and not the least stay curious as supervisor: "What is your (my) relationship to this . . .?" "If your (my) stomach had a voice, what would it say?" "How is it to talk about this, to hear yourself . . .?"

What I offered was an invitation for each one to articulate their feelings there and then, and then encourage the feelings to be expressed the way they wanted. I didn't see it as my task *to untangle the mess*, but rather create a space in which all the different relationships and feelings connected to the '*something*' could be expressed and acknowledged. This approach declines competition, and may generate a context where every expressed feeling is valid in its own right.

> I wanted the reflecting team as well as myself to be there for each one of the women, and let what they uttered touch us: to feel in our own bodies the sadness, loneliness, anger, frustrations that I could imagine Ellen, Lisa and Marion had been feeling.
>
> When I heard Ellen talk, I felt how she suffered the uttermost pain, and I could recognise an intense loneliness. I heard how she accused herself and was determined not to be spontaneous ever again. She felt so ashamed, she said, and it had been impossible to talk with anyone about what had happened, she didn't trust that anyone would understand how she had experienced it. Ellen also disclosed that she had been reluctant towards coming to the session today, she had even considered discontinuing her studies.
>
> Lisa talked about how she had felt blamed, and that had made her revisit self-contempt and accusations from others about being too clever. This was a recurring theme in her life, she said, the feeling of being too intensely concerned with what she felt was of great existential importance, while other people thought it was not that important. Lisa told how she too had been battling with shame of how she might have made Ellen feel inferior. That had not been her intention.
>
> Marion also spoke about shame, anger and about how she once again felt that what she uttered was not worth saying, remembering how time and again she has experienced being rejected after expressing herself. "When feeling safe, I show more of myself. But then I have experienced how this becomes 'too much' for people around me. I'm left with the feeling of people not being

able to put up with me, that I harm people by simply presenting myself. This creates guilt and despair. To present myself as open and explicit becomes a dangerous yearning." These feelings were not new, they were familiar to her, and she knew them from other contexts. Over and over, Marion dwelled on how she had reacted with feelings that were "more connected to previous experiences than to what was actually happening in the room and in between us, then."

Their talk struck cords in my own chamber of experiences. I could feel it in my breathing, how the warm salty water filled my eyes and how a big lump pressed up against my throat. I was *taking in* what was expressed, and I let Marion, Lisa and Ellen's agony fill me and meet my own bodily memory of loneliness, self-accusation, guilt and surprise.

When the reflecting team talked, they all gave something back after each round. The tone was serious as Susanne, Ida and Karen managed to express deeply what they felt: they acknowledged the feelings and told how they would have reacted in a similar situation. All three of them articulated surprise that the other had been so devastated. They were unhappy that especially Ellen had felt so utterly alone. They also pointed out that they were grateful for having a chance to hear about it now and that they hoped that this could make it easier for them to go on as a group. Maybe it even could strengthen the group culture.

We spoke for almost three hours using the time we needed for everyone to be able to talk at their own pace. It started out with a feeling of wariness, as if one might step on aching toes, but I could sense the tension loosen up as each one talked and could hear the voices of the others.

A new tone

We took a break, and then came back to have a less 'formal' format for talking. Sitting down, I felt I was in a new room, in a new group. Ellen was laughing and talking with Lisa about how the last weeks had been, but without the hesitation and guard I had felt was there in the morning. I wondered if the dark cloud of dejection and vigilance that had threatened to strangle this group of nice women was about to vanish.

The next day, we talked about other issues; about working in the mental health system, as a private practitioner and about concern for their own children and life situation. What struck me that day was the vibrant whole-hearted laughter that surrounded Ellen. She was not hesitant or holding back her spontaneity. It was a considerable shift in the atmosphere in the group. Most significant was that Lisa and Marion, who had mainly responded to each other the day before, incorporated Ellen in their talk.

Lisa was energised and pointed out that this experience was really worth something: "You showed us your work you know. We have really felt it, experienced how problems can dissolve when we talk about them like this. Rather phenomenal."

Letters from the supervisees

I asked the participants to write about their experience in the supervision, and send it to me. This was primarily for me to get an understanding of how they had experienced the supervision. But I eventually became intrigued by the opportunity this gave them, to dwell on the event and create questions and meanings that pointed beyond the supervision context.

Marion wrote:

> Permission is an important word for me, when I try to describe what opened up our dialogue. My experience was that you gave me permission to give an honest version without evaluating the content. At some point during our talk, you came up with a word that was too strong for me. A word I thought might hurt Ellen. It felt absolutely OK to correct your suggestion, and my reaction towards that word made it clearer to me what I meant.

The permission to talk, without being assessed or questioned, was, according to Marion, what made it possible for her to put words to her experiences.

This is not only about a particular moment; it is just as much an *overall atmosphere* of welcoming ambiguity, conviviality in the preliminary and temporarily, and how the supervisor poses questions and comments (e.g. "Was it like you were left all alone, or . . .?" where the word 'or' is pronounced not as a question that needs to be answered; it serves more as an invitation to consider possible alternatives).

Marion went on:

> It is always an act of balancing to take care of and develop the different relationships in a supervision group, and at the same time retain one's own integrity . . . But I think your questions and our dialogue invited us to take this into consideration, and challenge in all these directions. Your approach, being open and calm, and your considerations towards making your own expressions suitable for the other, is experienced as honest and inspires us to have confidence in you.
>
> I felt quite relieved the days after our talk. The feeling of loneliness connected to being in the group was experienced as less weighing me down. This physical feeling of being able to breathe easier was evident. It felt good when I managed to lower the guard.

Lisa wrote:

> I didn't prepare for what I should say or what should be my main message.
> I went right into the feelings I had had after our last session. Still, it took me
> by surprise that I all of a sudden felt that intense sadness I didn't have any
> control over. I could feel the tears coming, and that was OK. I felt a kind of
> compassion towards myself, not that I felt that sorry for myself, more a feeling
> of connecting to something important. I can't recall the questions Anne
> Hedvig asked, but I know that they were pointing towards an inner journey
> I was on. She didn't appeal to the memory, to make me recall what had
> happened. I think this was significant. It was more about my experiences,
> tied to who I am and what I have with me . . . Through this talk, and the
> questions Anne Hedvig asked, I managed to take this journey and worded
> some of the things that have been difficult in the supervision group. I believe
> I thought my fumbling came across fairly humanly, and that might have
> evoked a kind of empathy in the others. But not least, I managed to awake a
> generosity towards myself. I shouldn't need to be so hard on myself.

I believe not asking for recollections invited Lisa to talk about her 'inner
journey', her own relation to what had happened. Hearing herself, Lisa was
touched by her own voice (Andersen 1987) and she was able to hear herself as
someone she could care about. The feelings she had shown in the beginning of
our talk were guilt and shame. As we talked, these feelings were replaced by
compassion. This is the permission Marion wrote about, and maybe even more
strongly put, an invitation to express oneself without censorship. My questions
were presented in a tentative and fumbling manner, which might have invited Lisa
to fumble as well.

Lisa about listening to Ellen:

> When Ellen and Anne Hedvig talked, I realized that by listening to her
> experiences of the event, a whole new understanding emerged. I could hear
> her in another way. She was neither reproachful nor angry, which would have
> made me defensive. I could listen to her with the whole of me, and I could
> easily feel emphatic and even with more surprise, resonance. I think it would
> have been quite different if I had heard it stated with a double voice.

Now Lisa points at how she was able to hear Ellen's experience and emotion.
If Ellen had talked about 'anger', I believe I would have talked with her about
how she *relates* to her anger, not whom she is angry at or her reason for being
angry. In this way, I want to avoid resentment and defence in the group; instead,
a bridge might be built between the women.

Ellen wrote:

> . . . as I said, this was not something I had thought I would talk about. Then
> Karen and Ida commented on the episode, and it made me feel I should say

something, even if I felt reluctant to go into it. You made me feel safe and well looked after, and it was so nice talking with you, I nearly forgot the others. I was quite emotionally touched, since I felt I needed to talk about the pain. I felt I had ruined the nice chemistry in the group, and this created, as I told you, a feeling of guilt. I was overwhelmed by sadness; simultaneously it felt like a release to be able to talk about it. Because I hadn't talked with anyone and I believe it was because I felt I was the one to blame.

Ellen had felt all alone. My aim was to create a space where she could feel absolutely sure I would listen to her without judging.

Ellen continued:

As we talked and right afterwards too, I could feel how I calmed down, and the inner pain, the lump in my chest and stomach let go. I felt 10 kilos lighter when I went home. I had thought I was alone feeling bad about this episode, but when I listened to Lisa and Marion I understood how painful it had been for them as well. This was surprising; I thought it was just me. And I was also surprised when the reflecting team said that they hadn't understood how strongly I had reacted, and I had thought they all had thought I was the one to blame.

Ellen talked about the physical release, here in terms of a lump. I believe the lump appears when the breathing is held back, almost as if one has swallowed too much air to keep words from popping out. When Ellen's words came out, and were welcomed by the listeners, the lump evaporated.

Ellen continued:

As a professional, well I have a new understanding, we do experience situations differently. It is important to check out how and in what way people experience things. I also became interested in the meaning of words when I talked with you. I said something about 'go to war' and 'lay flat', and you remarked how these expressions were strong and asked me more about what I meant. This is something I will use in my work . . . Another thing that will have an influence on my work is that I, for instance, will not finish a conversation without asking if there are any 'stones in the shoe', which need to be attended to.

'A golden opportunity'

Two months later, we all sat seated around the same table. I started off by thanking the three women for their letters. This served as an invitation to talk more about what we had done the very first day we had spent together.

Susanne: "It was so important that this wasn't trivialised, that someone said 'don't think about it'. Instead it was, 'This was your experience, how was it for you?'"

Lisa: "To me, as part of this group, I believe we couldn't have gone on. I felt so relieved."

Marion said that if we hadn't talked about it, it would have hardened to heavy concrete. Now she felt relief, acknowledging that she had understood that no one wanted to harm anyone. To have this talk was timely; we could feel a sense of sharing the hurt.

Ellen: "You know, I could have quit, and the only reminiscence would have been the lump. I could have lived on and the only thing that would have been left from this training would have been a big lump. Instead, it was this sense of being met; that what was said was accepted, not questioned. We didn't unravel the event."

Lisa proposed: "This is something we can use in our own practice, this was a unique experience; just see what it did with us."

Karen: "This is gold you know, it is a golden opportunity – for us as trainees. To be able to feel all feelings. And to deal with it like this."

Ida: "Yeah, when we're invited to go into this, like we did."

This experience created an opportunity to reflect and understand that we don't need to unravel stories about shared events. When the supervisor acts into the here and now, he or she doesn't need to understand the 'underlying story'. He or she must rather trust the feelings he or she can see, feel and hear in each person and in him or herself. What was important for this group was to be able to talk without being evaluated. The supervisor's task was to support the building of an organic bridge between people who felt disconnected. A rupture in the group would have made it difficult to go on together. We managed to generate a dialogue that created opportunities for reconnection – not necessarily through agreement, but in acknowledging our emotional relation to what we had experienced. Just as the court in the Ethiopian province of Wollega grants everyone to be in his or her own right, in the shades of the mango tree.

Closing reflections and new beginnings

As supervisors, we have a treasure trove of opportunities if we use the present movements in supervision to explore inter-actions and intra-actions. I want to encourage supervision groups, the supervisor included, to become sensitive and responsive by encouraging a benevolent curiosity towards every new encounter. We should use all opportunities to learn by opening ourselves towards what emerges. This means that we must pay attention to the musicality of the present movements, sometimes to the expense of what is considered proper for 'clever' people such as therapists, supervisors or supervisees.

The modernist's spell, demanding coherence and consistency, is ever-present in supervision contexts as well as in therapy. People usually want to present themselves as valid and valuable, sensible and intelligible. This often creates an obligation to think and talk consistently and fluently, almost in the form of pre-rehearsed texts (Dreyfus 1979; Devlin 1997). My experience is that it helps supervisees to experience what is important if the supervisor repeatedly insists that "there is no need to be exact; it is the continuing and never-ending search *towards* meaning that is interesting." My point is to underline the potentials we have as we invite supervisees to dwell, connect with bodily sensations and acknowledge the not yet said but distinctly felt. What seems chaotic doesn't need to be narrated into coherent stories. Here, I call attention to a relational practice where fluidity and complexity are cherished over definitions and explanations, a space that calls for an orientation that I sometimes call *relational contemplation* and an invitation to *relational compassion*.

As supervisors, I believe we need to let ourselves become part of this fluid and complex space, where we are willing to loosen control and become emotionally available. I think we need to remind ourselves of being curious, redefining our position from expert to learner rather than teacher.

Notes

1   Einstein proclaimed his admiration for the physicist Niels Bohr by underlying a way of relating to knowledge and truth, by saying: "He utters his opinions like one perpetually groping and never like one who believes he is in possession of definite truth" (Pais 1991: 37).
2   These students are required to have 120/240 hours supervision during their two or four years of training. Since they live all across Norway, and need to travel to meet their supervision group, we often have whole-day supervisions, or even two-day sessions.
3   The program encourages students to have some variation in their supervisory experience by having more than one supervisor.

References

Andersen, T. (1987) 'The reflecting team: dialogue and meta-dialogue in clinical work', *Family Process*, 26: 415–28.

Anderson, H. (1997) *Conversation, Language and Possibilities*, New York: Basic Books.

Anderson, H. (2012) 'Collaborative relationships and dialogic conversations: ideas for a relationally responsive practice', *Family Process*, 51(1): 8–24.

Bakhtin, M. (1981) *The Dialogical Imagination*, Austin, TX: University of Texas Press.

Bakhtin, M. (1990) *Art and Answerability: Early Philosophical Essays by M.M. Bakhtin*, edited by M. Holquist and V. Liapunov, Austin, TX: University of Texas Press.

Bjørkvold, J.R. (2005) *Det Musiske Menneske*, 7th edn, Oslo, Norway: Freidig Forlag.

Devlin, K. (1997) *Good Bye, Descartes: The End of Logic and the Search for a New Cosmology of the Mind*, New York: John Wiley & Sons.

Dreyfus, H. (1979) *What Computers Still Can't Do: A Critique of Artificial Reason*, London: MIT Press.

Friis, P. and Larsen, H. (2006) 'Theatre, improvisation and social change', in P. Shaw and R. Stacey (eds), *Experiencing Risk, Spontaneity and Improvisation in Organizational Change* (pp. 19–43), London: Routledge.

Gendlin, G. (2003) *Focusing*, London: Rider.

Kapuscinski, R. (1998) *The Shadow of the Sun: My African Life*, London: Penguin Books.

Lipari, L. (2009) 'Listening otherwise: the voice of ethics', *International Journal of Listening*, 23: 44–59.

Malloch, S. and Trevarthen, C. (2009) 'Musicality: communicating the vitality and interest of life', in S. Malloch and C. Trevarthen (eds), *Communicative Musicality: Exploring the Basis of Human Companionship* (pp. 13–15), Oxford: Oxford University Press.

Morson, G.S. (1994) *Narrative and Freedom: The Shadow of Time*, London: Yale University Press.

Pais, A. (1991) *Niels Bohr's Times*, Oxford: Clarendon Press.

Seikkula, J. and Arnkild, T.E. (2013) *Open dialog i relasjonell praksis*, Oslo, Norway: Gyldendal.

Shotter, J. (2011) *Getting It: With-Ness Thinking and the Dialogical . . . in Practice*, New York: Hampton Press.

Stern, D.N. (2010) *Forms of Vitality: Exploring Dynamic Experience in Psychology, the Arts, Psychotherapy, and Development*, Oxford: Oxford University Press.

Vedeler, A.H. (2011) 'Diving into the poetic movements, exploring "therapy" and supervision', doctoral thesis, University of Bedfordshire, UK.

Wittgenstein, L. (1953) *Philosophical Investigations*, Oxford: Blackwell.

Chapter 5

Working at the extremes
The impact on us of doing the work

Helga Hanks and Arlene Vetere

He who fights against monsters must beware lest he become one himself. And when your gaze penetrates deep into the abyss; the abyss can penetrate deep into you.

(Nietzsche 1886)

Both of us (HH and AV) work systemically and psychodynamically as therapists, supervisors and organisational consultants, and have done so for many years. We were specifically interested in what happens when professionals are pushed to their limits in terms of what they listen to and experience in their practice. This includes working with the individual client but also with the wider system when trauma, abuse, hardship, overwork and violence are at the centre of cases. In this context, our approach to personal and professional development is both similar and different when compared with other therapeutic work. The difference is in how we help practitioners stay present, thoughtful, compassionate and creative when working at the extremes of human experience. Central to this is how we understand and almost withstand looking violence and abuse in the face. Thus, therapy itself is different. Safety is uppermost. Practitioners adopt a dual position of explanation and responsibility in their approach to those who do harm within a clear moral position of believing that people are entitled to live without fear of the people they love or who care for them. So staying compassionate and taking care of ourselves and others enables us all to carry on with the therapeutic work, thus giving a service to all people who need it (e.g. in our work with those who perpetrate harm and abuse). In addition, we also think of those who work in other areas (e.g. with severe illnesses, in accident and emergency services, forensic services and when people become carers (including children) of those who suffer from severe, debilitating conditions). Other areas of work have included those in military services or those NGOs working in conflict areas, when disasters have occurred, and areas of extreme health issues (such as the Ebola crisis in Africa) affecting both a population and those that come to help. In this chapter, we will concentrate on the areas of violence and child abuse. Last, but by no means least, we think of those who overwork, for whatever reason, whether they are work-addicted or pushed by, for instance, performance objectives, long waiting lists in the NHS and other stressful situations within organisations.

Our work is with all forms of abuse across the lifespan, including all forms of child abuse as well as child sexual abuse and interpersonal violence. We listen to harrowing stories, from our clients and from our supervisees. A vicarious experience of listening to and reading about such terrible events can also evoke a similar emotional response in the listener or reader. Importantly, we need to recognise that this includes participants in training workshops and also the administrative staff who type letters and reports for practitioners. The question of how we support administrators in these circumstances remains largely unaddressed in our health and social care organisations. Our supervisory work also includes guiding, mentoring and supervising colleagues working in the field, including supporting them when they have to appear as expert or clinical witnesses in family and criminal courts, complaint procedures and at times witnessing with families and colleagues the impact of emotional and/or physical abuse, such as the death of a child because of abuse, or the impact of being present when a family member is wounded or killed. In all aspects of our work, moral, relational and psychological aspects are primary, yet one of our highest context markers is always, and has to be, the legal system and the law.

It has long been recognised that working in the area of child abuse and violence is stressful. Many professionals are touched by the effects and its often insidious and slow process of impacting on the well-being of the individual. Both our working and private lives can be involved, more than we often wish to acknowledge. There have been moments along the way when we have felt either we could not listen further or when we have been overwhelmed with feelings of compassion. There have also been times when severe threats to our persons have created powerful emotions, including fear, disgust, moral opposition and so on. Consequently, learning to attempt to understand fear, or listen to, for instance, cruel and/or intimately distressing times in our clients' lives can have powerful consequences on our well-being. These responses are driven largely by a wish to protect, but at either extreme of responding, we are aware that our capacity for thoughtfulness could have been affected, leaving us subject to reactive responding. Thus, helping clients, trainees, supervisees, colleagues and ourselves to stay present, focused and reflective is our main aim, and to do that we draw on an integration of multiple theories and practices. These will be outlined in the following pages.

Case material

To illustrate some of the situations we have known, we will describe some case material first. We have decided not to describe here the most violent and abusive cases, though we have experienced as part of our casework, murder, severe physical injuries, operations of sex rings, ritualistic abuse and others. However, in order to protect the children and families involved, the cases will be constructed using aspects and incidences from a mixture of different family situations. We are creating a composite picture, to make specific points, but mostly to protect their anonymity and confidentiality. The case material stems from clinical work by clinicians working both in independent practice and in the National Health Service in the UK.

Example I

Working with a family in supervision, we realised with the supervisee the complex impact of many professionals becoming involved with the family after the abuse was discovered. We agreed that the supervisee would present a model of the family and professional system involved, as an eco-map, to the next multidisciplinary review meeting. To her surprise, some of the professionals became angry with her for presenting the material in this way and became hostile.

The supervisee became stressed (it was the unexpected hostility that created the feeling of stress) but people in the review meeting explained to her that they thought she laid the family open/bare for all to see how serious the case was. The family, present at the review, made a complaint to management, saying they had been exposed by this presentation. The family took a lead from other professionals and continued in their criticisms. Letters and leaflets were created by the family stating that this supervisee was incompetent and that he or she should be removed from his or her post. Management told the supervisee not to use such explicit presentation in the future. There were only a few professionals who said they found

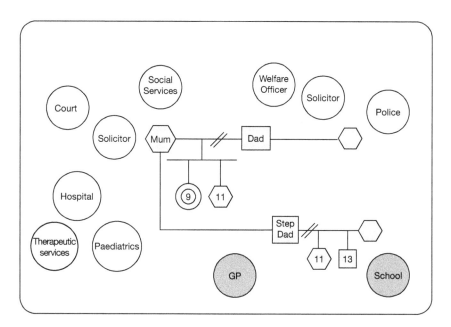

Figure 5.1 A family genogram and subsystems involved

it helpful to see the eco-map/genogram and how the family were suddenly the centre of so much attention.

On the face of it, this seemed such a simple task that had been performed in the interest of clarification of roles and tasks relating to the family and professional system. What subsequently ensued became distressing to the supervisee, involved many hours of writing letters, filling in forms, dealing with telephone and personal conversations, and contemplating dismissal.

In supervision, we discussed the following:

The supervisee was almost put in the same position as the abused child. It was his or her (the supervisee's) fault that the family had been exposed (to how things stood at that moment), in the same way as the child had been reprimanded by her family and told it was her fault that they had been investigated for abuse. The child had produced a drawing of her abuse.

In the supervision, which became much more frequent at the height of this case, we recognised the mirroring between the family and professional system. We also recognised that if everyone concentrated on the 'story of the professional eco-map/genogram', the 'story of abuse to the child' could be set aside, and even forgotten. Denial and a sense of fear of having to confront the issues may also have been present in the individuals and the system as a whole.

The supervisee stated that increased supervision and contact with the supervisor was very helpful. Making an appointment with management and discussing the case and the intention of the eco-map/genogram with professional systems to the family added was, the supervisee said, helpful.

As a supervisor, I felt at times I wanted to be closer to the supervisee and even see him or her outside working hours to support. In my own supervision, it became clear that though compassion and being frequently available in work time were essential, extending this to outside the working hours would possibly make us become enmeshed (cloud our judgement and possibly lose sight of the child and family, who are, after all, at the centre of this piece of work). What we did concentrate on was helping the supervisee to identify family members and friends who would support him or her at home and colleagues who would support him or her at work. We identified that it was unavoidable to think that the 'attack' on the supervisee could simply be forgotten once at home or in other work situations. So, to identify people he or she could trust in his or her private life was important. We also worked hard together in explaining eco-maps/genograms to other professionals (inside and outside the organisation the supervisee worked in) and management. We emphasised the helpfulness of these constructions and that they were not meant to do harm, but to achieve a clear and useful picture that was hopefully constructed to help the family and professional system (McGoldrick and Gerson 1985).

Example 2

Professionals were asked to visit a family. In preparation, they had been told that the family had a history of violence, but that one of the children had made a clear disclosure of abuse and it was imperative that more information was gathered and a conversation with the family was important. Two professionals arrived at the house of the family, but they found the garden gate locked and two large dogs racing to the gate with teeth bared. A member of the family came to the front door of the house and called out, asking what the two people wanted. When they identified themselves and said they wanted to talk with the family, the family member threatened them and said the dogs would be set on the two people if they did not leave immediately. In other instances, people have been threatened with physical violence, and threats of being harmed on their way home from work.

These incidences cause extreme stress, and on a continuum of responding can leave the professional at either end of the scale:

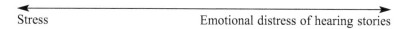

Stress   Emotional distress of hearing stories

Being a witness in therapy to the stories that both victims and perpetrators tell of the harm done to them and the harm they do, and their trauma responses, leaves the listener with an array of feelings, from compassion to anger to helplessness, and sometimes fear and resentment, as well as many other emotions. In the work as a supervisor, it has often come about that professionals have commented on the fact that their own sex life has suffered because of the terrible descriptions they hear, or as in the case of medical staff, injuries they have been witness to and had to treat. Talking about these topics in supervision or support is almost essential.

When small babies have been physically or sexually abused and neglected, it hits those working on the case particularly hard, especially so when they themselves have just become parents. Colleagues and those in supervisory and managerial positions should be aware that the professionals need protection for a time and have cases allocated to them carefully. However, it is also important that in the workplace, this should be discussed at all times and ways found to minimise the stress it can cause to staff. We remember the first time one of us (HH) stood next to a cot on a paediatric intensive care unit and watched a baby die from the effects of having had cotton wool put down her throat. We were all distressed, including the mother of the baby, who had done this because she had wanted to stop the baby crying. Sometimes there is very little difference between hearing the stories and being a witness to the discovery of an injury and its consequences.

Families, professional contexts and ecosystems

We are always reminded of Patricia Crittenden's (2002: 111) description of her experience with fostering children. She talks about the need "to ameliorate the interpersonal problems associated with child abuse and neglect." A difficult process we may say, and the dilemma is well described in her writing. The questions she asked of herself included, "Why did I not manage to help these children?"

When working and thinking around child abuse, we realise how important it is to consider the parts played by the people surrounding the child abuse – the families, the professionals and the organisations. In the pioneering stages of that work, we developed the idea of the jigsaw (Hobbs *et al.* 1999) as a way of making visible the systemic ideas that we felt were so important in seeing the children at the point of referral. This can, of course, also be created showing the professional system working with a family.

When we were thinking of the above with respect to writing this chapter, we created a *model of influence* as shown in Figure 5.2.

None of these systems will be left without the effects of the abuse spreading within each system and to other related ones. How each part of the larger system behaves will have consequences on the individual, their relationships and on society. Creating a systemic model can often be helpful in understanding the effects of anxiety in the system, the different contributions each of the 'players' make in what we have to deal with or why it seems impossible for the case to move forward.

We have always maintained that being able to predict a stressful event, even if one cannot control it, most often reduces the severity of stress and helps with de-escalation as we begin to understand and explain what is happening.

Models of trauma and trauma-organised systems are well described by Arnon Bentovim (1992), one among many of his publications. Among much of what he states, his perspective of society and the family is still today most apparent: "violence, incest and other forms of intra-family violence are not being seen as a symptom of a malfunctioning family but as a social and political problem stemming from patriarchal society's inability to protect victims" (p. xvii).

The cases relating to many cities in the UK where children are being trafficked (moved between places) and sexually abused by gangs of mainly male perpetrators, are still testament to the above in the twenty-first century. The investigations that are undertaken now in 2014 of cases of sexual abuse by high-profile citizens of this country (UK) are another example. This and many other failings to protect children make us think that we still have a very long way to go. Professionals need to take care to look after themselves at the same time as working and recognising these abuses.

Understanding the impact and consequences of stress in the workplace: compassion fatigue, burnout and toxic systems

As long ago as 1989, a colleague, Jeff Hopkins, said that he had listened to women social workers who were telling him that they felt stressed and that "they spend all day switching roles; working with families, foster parents, the children, the senior social worker, other agencies and at the same time being a wife and mother." We think this is transferrable to many professionals in health and social care and often works across gender. It is a powerful description of what can lead to

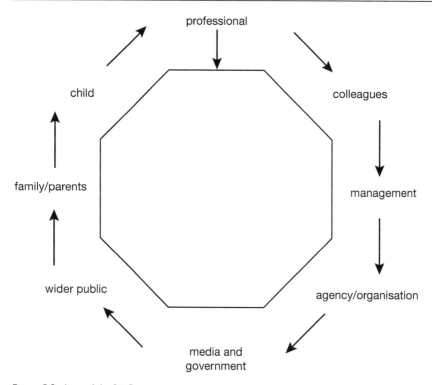

Figure 5.2 A model of influence

unwished for and unrecognised creeping symptoms of malaise that can affect our physical and emotional health.

Very briefly, the consequences from any form of stress in the workplace – from not enough/appropriate training (something we need to consider in the NHS/social care today with financial cuts and solutions that often put less qualified but cheaper staff into positions), lack of/poor supervision (see above), to overwork – each and all can lead to the following symptoms: tearfulness, anxiety, headaches, poor sleeping patterns, poor eating patterns (over/underweight), becoming irritable, suffering from lack of concentration, becoming physically and emotionally ill, to name but a few. These situations, if not attended to, can lead to much more serious outcomes.

There is an important parallel to recognise here:

- In child abuse, it is very clearly stated that prolonged, repeated maltreatment of the children has long-term consequences both physically and emotionally for the children.
- Working with burnout, compassion fatigue and stress, it is also recognised that it is the prolonged *repeated* stress that causes long-term physical and emotional harm.

Creating a work-life balance or blend is a phrase so often used as a necessity to look after oneself, but of course it is easier said than done. We return to PPD and protective solutions and systems later in this chapter, but here we shall consider the consequences of stress: compassion fatigue, burnout and toxic systems.

When talking with professionals about the range of feelings that can be provoked by abuse and violence, we remind ourselves and our professional colleagues to remember that:

- Strong, powerful feelings can be provoked by listening to or being involved in cases of child abuse, and family violence as in our case. It also applies when rescue workers do their work, or the military engage in combat situations, or professionals care for the seriously ill and dying. The professional can either be mobilised into being overactive or over-controlling.
- Or we can freeze in a state of paralysis, a state where we cannot think clearly, where we cannot stay flexible and where it becomes too hard to keep the protection of the child and ourselves in focus.

In both these situations, the needs of the children, the families and victims of violence are lost. Often, we end up feeling that we (the professionals) have to protect ourselves. Both the above scenarios can lead to clouded judgement and decision-making, and then errors in the process.

There is not so much written in the systemic literature on the phenomenon of burnout as an interactional and systemic process, interestingly, as mostly it is seen to be an individual process (e.g. as secondary traumatisation). Because the term 'burnout' originated in the phenomenon of rockets catastrophically running out of fuel, it can readily lead to thinking in mechanistic terms as an individual's private reaction. In this chapter, we try to consider 'burnout' in context, and in particular to think of it as a relational process, as discussed below. We want to thank Mark Hayward and Ros Draper for helping us to clarify that burnout can occur when people stop responding to feedback (personal communication). If burnout can be considered to be a relational phenomenon, then extra-systemic factors can also be taken into account (e.g. unsupportive working environments (Morrison 1993; Scaife and Walsh 2004), lack of task and role clarity, lack of appropriate supervision and so on). Morrison (2005) was particularly interested in this area and developed a model to emphasise the importance of empathic and reflective supervision to ameliorate and prevent burnout. He emphasised how the cycle of no or poor supervision leads to workers being less confident, less open and less sharing, and how this in turn leads to poor communication.

Thus, a lack of feedback or a lack of response to feedback can be bidirectional and can operate within and between different levels of an organisation or professional system. There is, of course, a sizeable literature focusing on burnout as an individual phenomenon and the consequences for the individual of being in such a position. Charles Figley (2008, personal communication, Brisbane,

Australia) believes that 'compassion fatigue' is a more accurate and helpful way of describing the process and the result of severe stress and overwork that can produce in people/professionals a state of ill health, both physical and emotional, that is crippling and takes time and treatment to overcome. Lamson *et al.* (2014) point out that compassion fatigue can be seen as an occupational hazard. They also hypothesise that if awareness is not raised among the workforce, it will almost invariably lead to "increased practice-errors and ethical breaches, decreased productivity, and absenteeism" (p. 107) and so on.

We would add that emails and phone calls and messaging late at night are also a sign of overwork and being overburdened with work and possibly anxious as a result. Lamson *et al.* (2014) discuss the particular difficulties those in military services experience and how this impacts on medical and therapeutic staff when they not only care for the wounds (physical and emotional) of those who have been injured in conflict, but also how they deal, or not, with the secondary traumatisation that often occurs in staff and themselves. Comparisons can be drawn when thinking about therapists working with the impact of abuse and violence in family systems and across the generations.

Compassion fatigue and secondary trauma

It seems that compassion fatigue is more openly recognised in those who care for family members with a chronic, debilitating illness and care workers who also have daily and often 24 hours of care of people. We suspect that children who become carers of close relatives also suffer from this fatigue, though there seems to be no mention of it anywhere.

When strong empathic feelings are provoked in a carer about the person they care for, they can often themselves become traumatised. Over time, this strong feeling of empathy may become exhausting for the carer and consequently develop in the carer becoming less able to be empathic. This is almost a defence. Once empathy has been exhausted, the carer is not able to continue. However, if they do continue, the interpersonal situation between carer and cared for could deteriorate rapidly and dangerously, with negative consequences for both.

Lamson *et al.* (2014: 109) clarify the distinction that occurs between compassion fatigue and secondary, or vicarious traumatisation. It is a useful distinction. While compassion fatigue grows out of deep feelings of empathy, it can also be exhausted and run out of steam, so to say. It leads to the inability to care.

Figley described *compassion fatigue* as becoming a danger when "People who work with, support and help, or live with, people who are experiencing stress and distress can become themselves very tense and think constantly about the suffering of those they care for. Over time that can reach such a state that the carer becomes traumatised." The condition is then a "secondary traumatisation" (Figley 1995: 1–20).

Figley (1999: 3–10) said succinctly that "it has become apparent that those who experience *indirect* exposure to a traumatic event (i.e. secondary trauma) endure similar distress and grief as those who experienced the event directly." Thomas and Wilson (2004) discussed empathy in the treatment of trauma and said: "Survivors of trauma bring to their treatment settings an emotional intensity and a level of distress that can put considerable strain upon a clinician's empathic sensitivity."

Burnout

Burnout has a somewhat different quality from compassion fatigue and secondary trauma in the way it develops and presents. It is a very serious state of ill health and can have long-lasting consequences. Burnout is thought to be a defence when people have been subjected to long periods of demanding interpersonal work, which strains the psychological capacities of a person particularly when this work is undertaken without, or with little, support (Jenkins and Baird 2002). The analogy of burnout comes originally from engineering, and there refers to rockets that, if not watched and managed and maintained, can burn so fiercely that they eventually burn out – run out of fuel with spectacular consequences. In people, a similar process can occur when they work so hard that they become physically and emotionally exhausted and are quite unable to continue (run out of strength and energy). The person may come to believe that there is no purpose to their work anymore and that they have no control. The person can become cynical and negative about most things, including their clients. Eventually, it includes the person too, who feels worn out and unable to accomplish. Efficiency and productivity diminish in the person. Alongside all of this, physical health problems can and do occur. The strength of all these symptoms varies from person to person, and it might also be considered that there are people who thrive on stress – but even here only 'up to a point'!

We want to return to the way that the origin of the term 'burnout' in rocket science can easily organise our thinking of it as a malfunction within the individual. Burnout can become a very mechanistic way of describing what can happen to people when they are overburdened with stress. It leaves the responsibility with the individual alone. In the literature and in practice, it is the individual who is identified as the subject of the condition and also the person who is thought to have the responsibility to do something about it. But burnout always happens in a complex web of organisational and interpersonal processes (e.g. when an American astronaut was asked what he thought about during the 10-second countdown to lift-off, he said he was thinking about sitting in the middle of 5 million components, every one of which had been chosen because it was the cheapest available)! While the final stage becomes apparent in its effects on the individual, it is worse than a mistake to conceptualise it as being caused by a deficiency or weakness of that person; it is unhelpful. We discuss blaming in the final section, and will come back to thinking of how this might be addressed in a more compassionate and systemic way. We take seriously the ways the history of the term and condition of burnout can be unhelpful, but feel that it is used so much, in all walks of life, that we cannot avoid using and discussing the label under the burnout rubric.

It is recognised that the condition of burnout can take a long time to recover from and, importantly, that it can alter a person's personality. For professionals and caring family members, including children as carers, a state of being can occur that mirrors the situation, reflecting back on to the caring person a feeling that they are to blame for the lack of change in the individual or system. They can often be left feeling that a failure to change the (family) system becomes the professional's/carer's fault. This feeling of 'fault' is often echoed in both the children and professionals. The children who have been abused so often state and feel that the abuse is "their/my fault" – thinking "If only I was nicer, if only I was a girl/boy, if only I had not said, if only I had told someone of the abuse . . ." In turn, this can lead to extraordinary stress both for the clients as well as for the professionals who work with them.

Today, it is much more acceptable, and even demanded (though by no means always achieved), that professionals have supervision for their work so that difficulties can be discussed and brought out into the open. One of us has been working with medical professionals for more than 10 years and is convinced that if professionals are given the opportunity to discuss their psychological and emotional experiences in their daily work, their equilibrium is more likely to be maintained. As described in Barbara Kohnstamm and Arlene Vetere's chapter (Chapter 6, this volume), this kind of supervision or PPD can also safely take place in groups (see also Anne Hedvig Helmer Vedeler, Chapter 4, this volume). However, it is well to remember that in many helping professions, and we include the medical professions, it is still seen as a failure if one seeks help personally, and often it is outright refused. We agree that not everyone needs psychological help, as people have other resources. It only becomes an issue when all there is available is that the professional believes and feels they have to endure, show they are strong and not seek help.

When compassion deteriorates and fatigue and burnout appear

Developing an attitude, a state of emotion that brings together compassion with some emotional distance, is in contrast to when professionals depersonalise situations and people. This includes having a blaming stance towards others, being indifferent to people's position/plight, disregarding what people say, being cynical and uncaring in the disguise of being caring. An example may be when people come to hospital having self-harmed or attempted suicide. There has been, at times, a way of treating these people by punishing, blaming and disregarding them as attention-seeking rather than attempting to help and understand their condition and circumstances (Schaufeli 1999).

It is not only at the level of the relationship between caregiver (the professional) and patient or client that an imbalance can occur (e.g. at such times when the professional is putting in much more effort into their clients getting well than their clients might do themselves). This can lead to exhaustion for the practitioner, and even burnout, if the same lack of reciprocity also occurs at the organisational level. Apathy becomes the defence against frustration.

The managers and organisational aspects

Both authors have been influenced by the work of Isabel Menzies Lyth, who, in 1988, wrote about 'containing anxiety in institutions' with a considerable understanding of systemic influences in organisations. The 'caring professions' are particularly vulnerable when we think of the NHS or social care services today. We wish to point out that managers of people in the caring professions may also fall victim to stresses that lead to burnout or compassion fatigue. An example may be when managers have to cut staffing in their service and make people redundant. Working with the staff members' stress of not knowing who will lose their job and being responsible for creating this situation and making the decisions can be distressing, particularly if it has to be denied that this will cause sleepless nights for the manager too (Boland 2006). Maslach and Leiter (2008) point out that there are six systemic sources present in burnout:

* work overload;
* lack of control;
* insufficient rewards;
* unfairness;
* breakdown inside a department; and
* when in a company or organisation a conflict of values occurs.

Lamson *et al.* (2014) echo many of the above thoughts and warn that an outcome of not attending to one's feelings of distress, grief or trauma may seriously impair the professional's ability and capacity to care for others. As already said, managers themselves can be affected when they have, for instance, to hand out redundancies and demotions to the workforce on a frequent/daily basis. It needs to be recognised that the adoption and the pursuit of organisational goals can lead to significant stress for all in the workplace, particularly if they are in conflict with what staff feel the organisational goals are.

As supervisors, we must be very attentive to the fact that the workplace can be a powerful instrument of stress to all concerned. We also need to keep an eye on how the organisation we work in conducts itself. How do we conduct ourselves when the organisation is visibly and intentionally hostile to the workforce, by, for instance, increasing workloads without additional resources, downgrading pay structures and/or disregarding workers' views?

The question we may ask ourselves is, if 'good enough' caring by parents (something we value and advocate) is necessary to bring up well-balanced children, and thus mirrored in generations of families, can it also be translated into caring teams and organisations? Do we think that the workforce can function energetically, positively and successfully if we do not have a caring, thoughtful system operating in the workplace? It can be said that many of us working in the 'helping professions' recognise that there is something in our own history, experience and personality that made us choose this work. To a greater or lesser extent, we have a need to help. Boland (2006: 24) said: "when we work in systems which are dysfunctional (often like the families we see) we feel powerless like the children in such families might feel. We recognise that the children in such families can become difficult, oppositional but also anxious and all of this largely because they cannot change anything in their family to make it better. They also often feel that it is all their fault."

If such a scenario plays itself out in the workplace, the professionals too will feel that they are powerless, that they are not heard and that morale is low. In such situations, the workforce may also come to behave badly, and feel mistrustful and anxious. It may be well worth thinking about how abusive and violent family systems can mirror themselves in professional systems.

What to do about it? Personal professional development and continuing professional development as a necessity

"In order to get the facts quickly, you have to go slowly." This was a written note that hung above one of the authors' (HH) desks at work for years. Once Kahneman's (2011) book on 'thinking fast and slow' was published, it became clear that understanding something of that distinction could help in the day to day effort to work productively. Similarly, AV, in her family violence intervention service, soon learned that working slowly and 'walking around' in difficult interactions in family relationships made it more likely that safety plans would work in helping families predict and prevent the violence (Vetere 2012). In our experience, there are several ways in which we can all approach creating a culture in which stress in the workplace is taken very seriously. Hanks and Stratton (2007) wrote about their experience over several decades, reflecting that being organised by a sense of crisis could be counterproductive. They describe how it was often patience and a determination to make a difference that helped them to stay the course and consider alternatives. AV concurs from her experience with the view that helping each other stay persistent and hopeful in the face of disappointment is helpful.

Another example came from Firth-Cozens and Payne (1999), who wrote that organisations cannot ignore the high levels of stress in their workforce. Positive input within an organisation or team included clear and direct communication, truly learning from mistakes (it has to be a real attempt to learn from mistakes, not a newspeak announcement type of step), good team leaders, and the good training that goes with it, and greater cooperation at the highest level so that this culture can filter through to other levels. Difficulties with and for 'seniors', and among 'seniors', can have astonishingly powerful effects on the stress levels of their staff. This is often not realised within an organisation, and senior staff can "greatly underestimate the effects, for better or worse, that they can have on others" (Firth-Cozens and Payne 1999: 79–91). We need to consider and acknowledge the tensions that can occur when organisations have to take responsibilities of working in the field of violence and abuse and with the population they are serving. This is particularly so when the workforce is divided in believing that certain situations can or cannot occur. In our supervision and consultation practice, we often explore how abusive and violent family systems can mirror themselves in professional systems. Boland (2006: 27) pointed out that the "usual individually oriented models of burnout can invite us to feel responsible and pathologised, because, mostly they fail to place proper emphasis on the role that systems play in the creation and maintenance of toxic workplaces." While she considers the more negative effects on some professionals who work within abusive systems, Figley (2008, personal communication) also suggested that rather than focusing on negative, dysfunctional problems, disorders and psychopathology, "we must balance these negative elements with a focus on altruism, compassion, resilience, success and thriving."

We do not wish to propose that other means of caring for ourselves are not equally important: eating well, drinking fluids during the working day, having rests, attending to free time activities such as sport, the arts, cinema, exhibitions and walks, to mention but a few.

What are the main responsibilities of the supervisor?

As we said earlier in the chapter, we supervise individual practitioners, groups of practitioners and teams. We offer consultation to service managers and policy developers.

We believe it is helpful for supervisors to share with their supervisees some ideas about their style of supervision and their supervisory role. It then becomes possible to discuss the acceptable and collaborative parameters for the supervision of trauma-focused therapeutic work. We try to create calm and reflective spaces for thinking, where indecision, reflexivity and action in the therapeutic work will be held in equal regard. This allows us to be clear about how accountability for behaviour and responsibility for action can be shared such that tension and anxiety in the face of uncertainty can be contained. Such containment promotes the capacity for creative thinking and effective problem-solving.

We think it is helpful to tell supervisees we will *always* ask about their personal safety and well-being (Vetere and Cooper 2008). This needs to be a natural part of the ebb and flow of the supervisory conversation. If it is mentioned for the first time in the context of a particular piece of therapeutic work, it can have the effect of unhelpfully raising anxiety rather than acknowledging safety and threat that runs through the therapeutic work. We pay attention to the emotional well-being of supervisees and the effect this work has on them. For example, when AV first became a grandmother, and was asked by her son and daughter-in-law to babysit her 2-month-old grandson, she took nearly 30 minutes to dress him in his stretchy 'babygrow' as she was frightened she would break one of his tiny fingers! Needless to say, her little grandson did not appreciate the length of time she was taking, and she herself had not realised how over-sensitised she had become to the possible fragility of little children after years of looking at photographs of, and working with, children injured by their family members. In addition, there may be moments when the work triggers unexpected memories that take everyone by surprise. We will be straightforward about our willingness to be supportive within the supervisory relationship and offer appropriate advice and referral for therapy as necessary.

In parallel with the above, we recognise these 'boundaries' to be the responsibility of the supervisor when personal issues impact on their supervisory work. We hold a commitment to trying to maintain a balance between getting overwhelmed (or frozen), on the one hand, or underwhelmed and potentially unresponsive, on the other. We seek supervision for our supervision on a regular basis and in line with current professional regulatory requirements.

Reflection, reflection and reflection again: 'beyond reflective practice'

In the remainder of this chapter, therefore, we include all forms of supervision in our discussion: individual, group, peer, CPD and PPD, and supervision of supervision. Our main responsibility in the supervision/PPD and CPD work is to create a 'safe enough' context within which challenging and emotionally difficult things can be said and be heard. Thus, our starting point is ourselves and our own reflexive positioning. In our personal supervision, we keep a number of self-reflexive issues open for regular review, such as the meaning of being a woman as in our case, as well as working with men in supervision as supervisors, supervisees, trainees and clients, by constantly reflecting on the relationship between our values, hopes and professional ethics, and the impact of our own family life and cultural nuances in our work. There are no direct answers as such, but the continuing debate and the commitment to keep talking around these meanings and how they dynamically shift and change over our life cycles keeps us alive to the impact of these issues for our supervisees and trainees in their work. Reflecting in groups, peer groups and small multidisciplinary meetings may be an answer and help in making the process more creative.

We look after ourselves by trying to hold a balance between the impact of the multiple demands on us and paying attention to emotional safety. This informs how we approach and structure our work with clients and colleagues. We believe we live in a complex system of recursive feedback loops where we all can influence, help and learn from each other. Sustained attention to acknowledging, appreciating and praising the intentions, efforts and achievements of others is key to building cooperative working environments within which creativity and therapeutic risk-taking can be found, contained and developed. Finding positions of integrated thinking, within which meaning, and the apparent lack of it, can come forth from the unsayable and the unsaid, and connect with emotion that cannot always easily be put into words, is part of the supervisor's responsibility. Working with clients can create very similar situations for the therapist, as it does for the supervisor, in their work with trainees and other colleagues.

Bradbury *et al.* (2010) have critiqued reflection exercises and how they are carried out, particularly in the health services. They pointed out that it was not only a lonely affair at times, but also used to make the workforce adopt views that suited the organisation rather than helped the individual gain insight and learn. Sweet (2010) pointed out that reflections, rather than being related to new learning and discovery about oneself, have in places become a 'checkbox exercise'. Reflections in systemic practice can be immensely useful particularly if created in conversations with others. It can change one's view. However, if the reflections are created in order to achieve an assessment or self-assessment exercise, the quality of the reflection has changed and is the less in quality as a result.

Creating a conversation that includes safety, doubt and progress

We often use the following format to structure a supervision session that is dedicated to the presentation of a specific dilemma or set of concerns around therapeutic work with a family. This format can be used in both individual and group supervision. We start by asking supervisees to describe the case from the family members' point of view, and from the agency's point of view. We speculate about what other descriptions the family members might want us to know about, and what other issues and descriptions of the family the team might want us to know about. We establish what the supervisee wants from supervision in terms of goals, and if family members could be present, what they would want from the supervision consultation. We enquire about what the family members are doing right, what is working well, and how the family members are trying to pay attention to safety. We enquire about the history of violence in the family and what action, if any, has been taken. We establish where there might be agreement and disagreement between the supervisee and their team (and/or the agency and the supervisor) about the level of risk of further violence and/or any action to be taken. And finally, we would ask: if the family members and other agency/team staff had listened to our conversation, what would they say?

Looking after ourselves as supervisors and practitioners: protection and growth

We are always striving to achieve a balance in life. So what does and could this balance look like? How do we do it? We make time for friends and family. We take time out for ourselves. We invite friends and family to give us feedback. We maintain realistic expectations and goals of what we can and cannot do in dialogue with others who know us well – and we listen to what they say! We teach and train and enjoy learning and working with colleagues who share our passion for helping individuals and families make things better. We learn and benefit from the families we work with, over and over again. We read relevant literature and others' ideas and ways of working, creating an open flow of information. We do not always work alone. We create opportunities for joint working, consulting, supervising and so on. We collaborate with other agencies and community groups, and spend as much time as possible on good networking and liaison work. We recognise that much of the work we do, even that described as 'firefighting', is actually preventative when considered in a systemic and relational context that focuses on corrective scripts for the future of children. And finally, we do not give up hope or the wish for connection. We support persistence in the face of disappointment, discouragement and 'not listening'. All these ideas and activities are mutually supportive in a recursive fashion over time and involve many people. We find that what we invest in terms of energy and commitment in our work comes back in manifold ways to keep us going!

This balance is the platform of well-being on which we offer supervision. Our supervisees need to know we practise what we preach. An activity we find helpful for both practitioners and supervisors is to interrogate what theoretical ideas we are most and least attracted to in terms of what implications those ideas have for promoting relational and personal safety in every respect. We do this on a regular basis as part of how we review the usefulness of the supervision process.

During our professional working lives, many of us might be living with others (e.g. partners, children, parents, friends and so on). Our decision to work with risks of harm and the effects of harm may have been taken by us without involving our 'nearest and dearest'. Even when we have their support and understanding for our professional work, our decision to focus in this area and the unrelenting nature of its impact will affect them too. For example, if we cannot sleep at night, or wake up worrying about a family, the person sharing our bed and those living with us will know. So clearly, we need to include them in our thinking, both self-reflexively and for our supervisees. So we wish to highlight and honour their support in enabling us to keep going. In our experience, our partners have been our 'stable fourths'! In the triangle between ourselves as supervisors, our supervisees and their clients, our partners have often helped us stabilise these working triangles with their quiet commitment and understanding. In the creation and maintenance of stable triangles of interaction, we are able to think reflexively and clearly, to actualise support and to make our best decisions.

Beware the blame

Last, but not least, a word about blame, or rather 'not to blame' might be appropriate here. In much of our work, when we have been challenged, often to a high degree, and when our supervisees have been similarly stressed, the question about whether we are strong enough, good enough, clever enough and so on comes to our mind. When talking with professionals recently, we discussed this feeling. Should we be able to withstand all pressure, be professional and behave as if unaffected by what has been put our way? Medical colleagues will be particularly aware that they need to be seen to be taking everything coming their way with a strength that is almost superhuman – which, of course, they are not. We discussed the consequences of this earlier, and yet people often feel to blame, or that they are weak, when they are not able to cope. Other professionals may feel they have a right to blame these same colleagues and label them as weak. We want to make a plea that blaming someone who has suffered or is suffering from work-related stress, compassion fatigue or worse is unprofessional, unacceptable and deeply unhelpful, hindering the recovery of the person in question. The person suffering from stress-related conditions has usually done work beyond the call of duty. The organisation has to take a good look at itself if people fall victim to these conditions. It is the repetitive aspect of our work that can be the issue (e.g. abuse and violence seen again and again). What happens when we need to draw on our resilience again and again and again, and at times are not able to feel that we have any resilience left? Become sick or unable to continue? Are we to blame? Is this a flaw in our character? We think not, definitely not. Colleagues and the organisations we work in and for need to be mindful of this scenario. Sometimes, people need a rest and should not be punished if they are off sick for a time.

In conclusion: dilemmas for practitioners

To summarise: there are many dilemmas for practitioners who work therapeutically with interpersonal violence, trauma responses and trauma-organised systems. They risk being overloaded with information without finding clarity. Tensions can arise from constantly being asked to judge unpredictable behaviour. Practitioners can become isolated through not sharing their concerns and their resulting preoccupation with the family. There can be many reasons for not sharing concerns, not least a fear of being judged as incapable or incompetent. Sometimes, practitioners are being sidelined and criticised for working in areas that are seen as 'not nice', controversial or perceived as wrong and not 'our' (professionals') business.

In these contexts, practitioners can lose sight of their own competencies and resilience, and seek simplistic solutions in an attempt to manage overwhelming complexity and anxiety, both their own anxiety and that of others. Regular exposure to others' distress and the impact of harm can lead to over-empathising with the victim and repeating a cycle of victim/rescuer positions, with the resulting frustration and anger over agency responses, services and management decisions.

We have, in this chapter, talked about difficult aspects of our work in clinical life and in supervision. Many of the theoretical and philosophical points have been discussed in detail in other chapters in this book (see Jim Sheehan, Chapter 8, this volume), and we have concentrated here more on the practical side of our work. Our aim has been to speak about some of the difficulties that we know from experience practitioners have to deal with on a day to day basis when they work with child abuse and intra-family violence.

References

Bentovim, A. (1992) *Trauma Organised Systems*, London: Karnac Books.

Boland, C. (2006) 'Functional families: functional teams', Australian and New Zealand Journal of Family Therapy, 27(1): 22–8.

Bradbury, H., Frost, N., Kilminster, S. and Zukas, M. (2010) *Beyond Reflective Practice: New Approaches to Professional Lifelong Learning*, London: Routledge.

Crittenden, P. (2002) 'If I knew then what I know now' in K.D. Browne, H. Hanks, P. Stratton and C. Hamilton (eds), *Early Prediction and Prevention of Child Abuse*, (pp. 111–26), Chichester, UK: John Wiley & Sons.

Figley, C. (1995) *Compassion Fatigue: Coping with Secondary Traumatic Stress Disorder*, New York: Brunner/Mazel.

Figley, C. (1999) 'Compassion fatigue: toward a new understanding of the costs of caring', in B.H. Stamm (ed.), *Secondary Traumatic Stress: Self-Care Issues for Clinicians, Researchers, and Educators* (2nd edn) (pp. 3–28), Lutherville, MD: Sidran Press.

Firth-Cozens, J. and Payne, R.L. (1999) *Stress in Health Professionals*, Chichester, UK: John Wiley & Sons.

Hanks, H. and Stratton, P. (2007) 'On learning from the patience', *Clinical Child Psychology and Psychiatry*, 12(3): 341–7.

Hobbs, C., Hanks, H. and Wynne, J. (1999) *Child Abuse and Neglect* (2nd edn), London: Churchill Livingstone.

Jenkins, S. and Baird, S. (2002) 'Secondary traumatic stress and vicarious trauma: a validational study', *Journal of Traumatic Stress*, 15: 423–32.

Kahnemann, D. (2011) *Thinking Fast and Slow*, New York: Allen Lane/Penguin Books.

Lamson, A., Meadors, P. and Mendenhall, T. (2014) 'Working with providers and healthcare systems experiencing compassion fatigue and burnout', in J. Hodgson, A. Lamson, T. Mendenhall and D.R. Crane (eds), *Medical Family Therapy* (pp. 107–24), New York: Springer.

McGoldrick, M. and Gerson, R. (1985) *Genograms in Family Assessment*, New York: W.W. Norton & Company.

Maslach, C. and Leiter, M. (2008) 'Early predictors of job burnout and engagement', *Journal of Applied Psychology*, 93: 489–512.

Menzies Lyth, I. (1988) *Containing Anxiety in Institutions*, London: Free Association Books.

Morrison, T. (1993) 'The emotional effects of child protection work on the worker', *Staff supervision in Social Care*, Hove, UK: Longman.

Morrison, T. (2005) *Staff Supervision in Social Care*, Hove, UK: Longman.

Nietzsche, F. (1886) *Beyond Good and Evil*, Leipzig, Germany: C.G. Naumann.

Scaife, J. and Walsh, S. (2004) 'The emotional climate of work and the development of self', in J. Scaife (ed.), *Supervision in the Mental Health Professions* (pp. 30–51), Hove, UK: Brunner-Routledge.

Schaufeli, W. (1999) 'Burnout', in J. Firth-Cozens and R.L. Payne (eds), *Stress in Health Professionals* (pp. 17–32), Chichester, UK: John Wiley & Sons.

Sweet, J. (2010) 'Beyond reflection dogma', in H. Bradbury, N. Frost, S. Kilminster, and M. Zukas (eds), *Beyond Reflective Practice: New Approaches to Professional Lifelong Learning* (pp. 182–91), London: Routledge.

Thomas, R. and Wilson, J.P. (2004) *Empathy in the treatment of trauma and PTSD*, New York: Brunner Routledge, Taylor & Francis Group.

Vetere, A. (2012) 'Supervision and consultation practice with domestic violence', *Clinical Child Psychology and Psychiatry*, 17: 181–5.

Vetere, A.L. and Cooper, J. (2008) 'Supervision and family safety: working with domestic violence', in J. Hamel (ed.), *Intimate Partner and Family Abuse* (pp. 347–60), New York: Springer.

Chapter 6

A supervisor's progression

From personal and professional development training in group settings to the inclusion of the self of the therapist in supervision

Barbara Kohnstamm and Arlene Vetere

This chapter is based on a conversation between Arlene and Barbara about Barbara's experience of developing and facilitating personal and professional development groups for master's level trainees in systemic psychotherapy, while Barbara was living and working in Dublin, Ireland, on both the Clanwilliam (2002–2010) and University College Dublin/Mater Hospital (1996–2001) training programmes. Subsequently, Barbara moved back to live and work in The Netherlands. Here, she offers 25 session 'training psychotherapies' to systemic psychotherapy trainees either during their training or upon completion of their training. In addition, she currently supervises mature systemic and Rogerian psychotherapists. Reflections on all these experiences constitute the conversation, integrated in the context of our long-standing collegial relationship.

In this chapter, we hope to recreate the shared and personal nature of the conversation for Barbara, and as such will use the first-person pronoun to represent Barbara's views and experiences as she reflects on her progression.

Introduction

In this conversation, I, Barbara, would like to say something retrospectively about the value of having PPD as part of the professional training of systemic therapists, whether done as a group process as part of the training or as a time-limited 'training psychotherapy' during the course of a training programme or upon completion of a training course in systemic therapy. I would like to reflect on the challenges and benefits I experienced having facilitated PPD groups at both institutes in Ireland, and on some of the benefits I experienced meeting trainees in what we in The Netherlands refer to as individual 'training therapy', in which a partner and family members are at times invited to participate.

Second, from my present practice as a supervisor and trainer in systemic therapy and in emotion-focused couple therapy (EFT) (Johnson 1996), I will describe how in these last six years, I have introduced the personal story of the supervisee as a natural part of supervision, with some short examples of how and why the personal was addressed between the supervisor (myself) and the supervisee.

I have come to see this personal element as a crucial cornerstone of my supervision and will say more about this later in our conversation. Thus, this chapter reflects my learning about the significance of emotion and emotional safety as I journeyed from facilitating PPD in training groups to supervising mature and experienced therapists.

What were some of the challenges you encountered while establishing and facilitating PPD groups in Ireland?

I will respond to this with a series of questions as they encapsulate the dilemmas and challenges we grappled with as a staff training team in our early days of establishing PPD training groups, and in articulating them here, I hope the reader will then see how we addressed and resolved many of them.

For example, at that time, we asked each other: How do we as a staff team and trainers, with a 'duty of care' responsibility to both trainees and the public, deal with confidentiality within PPD groups and within the faculty? How do we raise discussion of emotion and attachment in a safe enough way in the PPD groups? How do we develop systemic practice and thinking within an educational model so students/trainees feel respected as adults, but also take responsibility for the feedback they receive, and recognise they are in a learning situation? How can we develop a coherent PPD model so the above is true, and at the same time we acknowledge that within the training team, there are positions of power and authority that we hold? These are the questions we asked ourselves and each other as faculty colleagues during my time of PPD group facilitating in Ireland.

The question is often asked as to whether the PPD group facilitator should be someone who is part of the training team but not a direct supervisor, or an external facilitator? However, some training programmes require the clinical supervisor to do the formal PPD training so there are no secrets, splits or 'cut off' parts, as best as can be achieved. If the facilitator is part of the training team, though, I think it needs to be crystal clear for the participating trainees what is being brought to the training team from the PPD groups, and how these lines of communication run. From the trainees' perspective, the tension between wanting the group to be a safe place, on the one hand (i.e. a therapeutic space where they learn a great deal from each other and within themselves), but, on the other hand, to recognise that the anxiety is always there as to how this will reflect on them within the group now, and within the training team and on them all later as colleagues. The invitation within the PPD group to go deeper into the sharing of our humanness is set against the sense it is a part of an evaluative arrangement within the context of a professional training in which they are constantly being assessed.

These questions reflect the organising principles of PPD groups and how they are situated within training programmes. In addition, I think raising these questions within a faculty team and examining the dilemmas within these principles constitutes an intervention into the functioning of the training team. The interesting and challenging thing about PPD group work is that if you become too strict and tight (i.e. completely confidential), it risks becoming un-systemic (i.e. what if things happen in the PPD that are very much linked to the challenges for a trainee and/or within a supervision group) – it makes it important that some conversation can take place within the wider faculty team and with the trainee, albeit with some protections (i.e. permission and transparency).

In PPD groups, we are asking trainees to take emotional and relational risks (e.g. sharing their thoughts and feelings about their lives, their childhoods, their stories, and their feelings about their clients). Trainees are invited to share their reflections with each other, yet at the same time they are part of a training where they are being evaluated – they get pass/fail marks in other parts of their training. These trainees could, and do, end up being colleagues in local teams, and most importantly part of the same professional group for the rest of their careers.So any personal disclosures or uncomfortable moments stay in the collective memory. I think these are the parameters within which we need to think as trainers and PPD group facilitators.

Why does a PPD group need such safety?

A sense of emotional safety is needed in PPD group work because you are asking people to reflect on and think about their attachment histories (i.e. to talk about the ways that they grew up in their families). For example, group members might talk about the death of a husband who revealed an affair when on his deathbed, or talk about the loss of trust, or talk about growing up in a children's home because your mum let all 12 of you go, or poverty and alcoholism, or incest in your family, or mental illness, severe handicaps, physical violence, despair and suicide. If someone goes to a therapy group, they go by their own choice because they think they recognise their pain and the need to work that out, along with people who have also all sought help – all kindred spirits. This can provide a huge sense of safety as all these people have declared, "I am not doing well." When the therapy group is over, we might never meet again, *but* in the training group, we will see each other again in our future careers, and we may have no common sense of having shared problems, but rather a need to be seen as competent and thus being without problems. If we feel embarrassment or shame, and uncertainty about sharing, we may doubt it will be understood and met with understanding and acceptance. It seems there is more scope for PPD group members to sit on the fence in a PPD group, with more reluctance to engage. I see the enormous value of PPD group work in the unfolding of stories behind our personal and professional identity. PPD work can create greater understanding of how we human beings are influenced and formed in the context we grew up in, and made sense of the world as we experienced it. It will help shed a light on places we were afraid of or ashamed about. It will also help narrow a false sense or division between our clients and ourselves as human beings.

The PPD group facilitator needs to be present, attuned and inviting in order to say, "What's going on for everybody?" The facilitator helps to distil the essences of experience, and to stay constructive. They function as a moderator all the time, trying to balance it with not interfering too much (i.e. talking too much and/or making too many interventions) while giving space for group members to develop their own sense of professional identity and bring their current concerns.

What are some of the influences on your practice as a PPD group facilitator?

I have been influenced by Yalom (1995) in his work with groups. I was supervised by a group analyst influenced by humanistic and systemic models. This has helped me realise the importance of linking group members' experiences (i.e. linking across common experiences within the group). This avoids shame and shaming, and however the PPD group is run, it has to be as congruent as possible to the model of psychotherapy practice being trained in, otherwise it can be too confusing for group members. If it is not theoretically congruent, it makes it harder for trainees to predict what might happen and creates too much uncertainty. I think there has to be a certain level of transparency (i.e. being clear about the structure and format of the group), thus 'knowing where you are'. The structure provides enough safety/secure base to explore the unpredictable, and the associated feelings of uncertainty. The group facilitator is the tone setter, modelling a certain amount of openness, and can be straightforward about talking about difficult moments. The facilitator is also the group historian who remembers how the last group session went, and how it ended. This is followed closely and carefully. The facilitator has the responsibility then to invite the more silent people to take part.

Reflecting back on my PPD work in Ireland, I realise that I remember the issues more than my role, and thus recognise that we need a process memory and to function as a process consultant. Many themes can arise for trainees in PPD groups. Social comparison is both a strong theme and tendency within PPD groups, often expressed as fear (e.g. am I better or worse than my PPD group members?). Forms of rivalry and judgements, prejudices, experience of injustice, sensitivities based on traumatic experiences, survival strategies, resilience, shame and guilt, and religion and beliefs have all featured throughout my PPD group work.

Compassionate appreciation and transparency in functioning create the context for safe self-evaluation and for hearing feedback from others. This offers an emphasis on formative feedback rather than summative educational evaluation. How is this self-evaluation done? There is much preparation before the PPD group evaluation as trainees are invited to say what they have learned during the training, in the group, and how they use it and make sense of it. They are asked to consider how they feel about their participation, what they are happy about/unhappy about, what else they need to pay attention to in their learning and development, and how they will get support for that. I invited other group members to give them verbal feedback in a reflecting format, and of course the feedback could be written up and given to them as well.

What are your ways of working with PPD during training, supervision and post-qualification practice?

I work with pictures, with objects, with sculpting and with themed days in the PPD groups. I consider one of the main beauties of systemic training to be the use of the genogram and all the ways in which we can encourage trainees to think about what formed them in their growing-up years (Hildebrand 1998). The genogram can track the social/emotional history of the family of origin and current family and/or can focus on the culture of origin genogram (Hardy and Lazloffy 1995).

Rodolfo de Bernart's work in Florence with photographs and images has been influential for me, so, for example, in presenting their genogram to the PPD group, group members might be encouraged to bring in images and photographs of themselves and their relatives. In genogram work, you can use symbols and small objects to represent and unlock implicit memories. People tell different stories about the same people, relationships and events when using objects to stimulate narrative production. Trainees are free to bring in their own objects, or I provide a choice of little objects from my 'treasure chest'. In my own life, I struggled with my relationship with my younger sister, whom I experienced as a rival for our mother's and father's attention. As adults, our relationship remained fraught, and then I attended a workshop where family photos were being shown to each other. To my amazement, my photo of us as four siblings sitting on a step revealed my younger sister's arm around my shoulder. I showed the photo to my younger sister, and asked if I wasn't hated as much as I thought for being such a nasty older sister. This started a whole new exploration for us together with a happy ending.

Another PPD activity popular with me is Per Jensen's exercise (personal communication, see Chapter 3, this volume) – a group member tells a story of their childhood and then tells a story of their professional life. The storyteller can face away from the group while telling the stories, if they wish, as a way of staying focused. The PPD group members are asked to find connections between those two stories in a reflecting team format, while the storyteller listens without commenting. When the group reflections are finished, the storyteller comments on those reflections.

I always think about Per Jensen's work and how he makes links with people's narratives about their own lives, and how they present their work to others, in supervision. PPD groups are the first place in a training programme where room is being facilitated to do that kind of linking, reflecting, and feeling (Hildebrand and Speed 1995). This is where the seed gets sown that however skilful and knowledgeable we are being trained to be, we are after all human beings, and that link is made in PPD more than in supervision, skills training, literature studies and so on.

The move to The Netherlands

'Training therapy' is a requirement in The Netherlands for all trainee systemic therapists. While we might say they lose out on some of the richness of being part of a group process, I have also seen that the safety of having individual sessions in which to address issues completely separate from the training institute has its advantages as well. The trainee is encouraged to bring in a spouse, partner, family member, children, sibling(s) or parents, as appropriate, to the sessions. This means that most of the trainees I saw had an experience of being in a session or having several sessions with some members of their own private context, which, after all, is what they will also do with their clients.

How do you address 'the self of the therapist' or our 'inner dialogue' in your supervision practice?

In this latter half of the chapter, I shall draw on my more recent experiences of providing supervision to more experienced therapists. We all know that there are times when, as therapists, we get triggered by our clients' issues or dynamics. There are times when our own internal emotional responses or reactions to what clients share with us in the session can get in the way of staying fully present with them. And these are the times when we need to think on our feet to try to make sense of our own sudden or intense reactions to a client so that this response can be digested and used in a therapeutic way.

I like referring to this process as 'the internal dialogue of the therapist'. In psychoanalytic literature, this is referred to as transference and countertransference. Since the time of Freud, the inner experience of the therapist has been given attention, and 100 years later I see this as one of the most important areas for therapists to develop their ability for free reflections and responses (i.e. free reflections rather than constrained, ignored, minimised and/or ashamed). In the systemic literature, this is called parallel process, resonating with the system or even becoming part of the system. In EFT, it is sometimes called 'getting caught in the negative cycle'.

It has always seemed to me that supervision needs to be safe enough to have the kinds of conversations where the personal reverberations/resonances of the supervisee could be brought into the room, without the supervision session turning into a therapy session. This makes room for the inner experience any therapist might have while conducting therapy, and is conceived of as a combination of bodily feelings and awareness, emotions, and thoughts, intentions and debates (Casement 1985; Satir 1987; Flaskas 1996; Rober 1999; Flaskas *et al.* 2005).

There seem to be different layers to which these inner dialogues can refer: On a professional level, we may ask, "What shall I do now in terms of the model?

What intervention to use? Or what is happening in this system?" On a personal level, we may ask, "What shall I do about these particular emotions or feelings I am experiencing in the session or afterwards? What can I do to make sense of these emotions in a safe way, in the heat of moment?" A therapist may simply realise he or she has encountered something that needs to be explored more after the session, either by him or herself, or with a supervisor or in peer consultation, or if needed, with a therapist.

In supervision, I used to wait for these more personal conversations to evolve when something in a therapy session triggered either the supervisor or supervisee to want to explore this internal dialogue. At that point, however, because we were already in the midst of it, usually a supervisee had felt stuck or ill at ease about something, and it seemed already to have caused some disturbance or some level of feeling stuck.

Can you give an example?

For example, one day, I challenged a supervisee, Juliette (a pseudonym) about my sense that I was under too much pressure to give her more than I felt I could in the time we had.

Juliette herself struggled with giving so much of her time and attention to clients who always seemed to need more and more of her time and attention and availability, and who were genuinely also often in serious trouble psychologically. I also saw her at times struggle to draw a line, or to bring up issues around boundaries with a couple whose 16-year-old daughter was still sleeping in the same bed as her dad and stepmother.

Looking back, I think she triggered in me an old feeling something like: "I am giving you all I can, and it is still not good enough?" So there certainly was a parallel process here, and I should have had a consultation with a colleague/supervisor about my feelings before addressing this with Juliette.

I also was very fond of her and saw her great strengths as a therapist. But I experienced Juliette as quite a challenge for me. I decided I needed to talk to her about my experiences with her. The conversation we had was painful for her and for me. I lacked sensitivity and was too blunt with her in addressing these issues that had arisen for me with her. She felt told off by me.

The next time she came, she said, "My training therapist asked me to ask you why you never asked me about my personal background?" I blushed and did ask her: her childhood was in the late 1970s when, in The Netherlands, a great deal of communal living experiments were happening with a great lack of clarity around boundaries. My supervisee found growing up very confusing and often still felt unsure of what was appropriate for her to do, say or ask and what was not, and she struggled with this. We worked on her own inner dilemma, as a therapist, of what was enough and what may be too much, for the remainder of her supervision. I am thankful to her for having shown me a missing link in my practice as a supervisor. If we had had the personal framework to have these conversations from the beginning, I am sure it would have been very helpful for both of us to put her behaviour in context and deal with it collaboratively.

That day was the day I decided that I wanted to ask all my supervisees to tell me something about their own life story and about possible triggers in their work with clients around 'raw' spots in themselves.

What changed?

It seems so obvious now, I am almost embarrassed that it took me this long to come to this place. It is as if up until that moment, in spite of me having been a PPD facilitator for many years, and in spite of having spent many hours in training therapy with trainee therapists, I still was not integrating the personal and professional aspects in my own style of being a supervisor.

I started to talk about this with my supervisees, asking them all, "What do you think would be good for me to know and understand about you and your own history, fears or pains, so that when these get triggered in your work, we both already have some idea of these issues? Might it be helpful to have a brief conversation about this now, or would you like to think about this question and tell me the next time?" I have started to ask this in the first supervision session, as well as with those therapists who already were in supervision, either individually or in groups.

I realise that it is not so much about the telling of all of the many details of our lives; rather, I think asking the question sets a tone and hopefully creates permission to go into the more personal domain when needed. It normalises the fact that, after all, it is our very resonances that hold important information for our clients as well as ourselves. So when do I zoom in on the personal aspects? If the supervisee tells me or if I have a sense that he or she feels unsure, unhappy, dissatisfied or stuck in the therapeutic work he or she is doing, that is when we try to search for the patterns that connect.

How did you progress from there?

In these following examples, therapists have brought their own personal blocks or automatic patterns into awareness, thereby freeing them to attune more fully to clients and address these issues in their own lives.

One supervisee, Rachel (a pseudonym), answered my opening question and said, "Well, I was so much the protector of my mother and I was her confidante. I saw her unhappiness with my father's unfaithfulness and her concern for my disabled brother. So as a young girl, I felt a great need to help her, to be on her side so as not to burden her, and not make things worse for her."

We were watching a video of her therapy session where a young woman finally chose to talk about having been unfaithful to her partner. She is very brave and wants to share with her partner how guilty she is feeling and how she knows this had hurt her partner. I saw Rachel turn very quickly to the partner, moving away from this brave and courageous wife. I asked Rachel, "What happened?" She said, "I don't know. I couldn't bear to stay with this vulnerability and opening up of the woman and felt I needed to protect her. So I turned away from her and talked instead to the husband."

We linked how she had felt such a need to protect her mother when she was young to her automatic tendency to protect her client from experiencing and expressing her pain and guilt. In making this link, she recognised that she did not have to do this in the same way anymore. She could be comfortable to support this woman to say some important things to her husband, which would help them heal and rebuild the trust between them, and that helping her to share openly was actually the most 'protective' thing Rachel could offer. In a subsequent session, she did beautiful work in processing the aftermath of the affair for both partners.

This theme of the supervisee needing to protect her clients from feeling too much pain or becoming too vulnerable has been a thread through the work this supervisee did. At times, she felt quite insecure about her own capacity for change. From watching parts of video clips, we both saw a gradual change and her increasing self-confidence. I saw her become very brave and I saw her ability to move in very close to the therapeutic edge. I saw her clients respond with increasing unfolding of a new kind of intimacy between them as a couple, having been encouraged by Rachel to share important issues together. I have felt very moved to have been invited in to be part of this process with Rachel, as her clients were moved by the changes in their relationship.

Another therapist, Jeanette (a pseudonym), says in answer to my question about her possible triggers, "My mother was in a concentration camp. So whenever there is a client whose parents were in a concentration camp, I feel great empathy with this person, and at times align myself too much with them."

But later, she said, "I have been thinking about your question. It is more complicated than that. The husband in this couple reminds me of my own husband; I love my husband very much but he can be such a bully and my children suffer. None of us can address this with him. He will not allow us to talk about the impact his behaviour is having on me and the family, and so we all walk on eggshells around him. This man in the couple does the same. I feel blocked and afraid to go there with this client and his wife. Now that I have seen how I get blocked with this client, I know two things more clearly: I must try and find a way to talk to my own husband and I will try and not shy away from this man in my couple. I feel less blocked now."

In subsequent sessions, the therapist was able to explore with the husband in this couple how, as a young boy, he had suffered from his own bullying father, and how he had sworn he would never end up being a bully like his own father, and here he was, being told by his wife that at times he was just that. He found it almost unbearably painful to feel these feelings.

It took a lot of sensitivity and courage on Jeannette's part to get permission to walk around this painful place, however briefly, with the husband. Both supervisor and supervisee concur that without having identified this parallel in her own life, she would not have been able to effectively attune to her clients and to explore these emotions and stay so connected both with the husband and the wife.

The third supervisee, Irma (a pseudonym), asked me to watch a session on video with a couple in which she said, "I cannot put my finger on it, but I am not happy with how it went." During the session, the wife expressed anger at her husband's behaviour. The therapist spent a great deal of time trying to understand why the wife had been so angry. The wife very patiently answered her several times. I could see from watching the video clip that the therapist could not attune to the wife as well as she usually did. The husband tried to come in from time to time, but the therapist did not seem interested to let him come in. At the end of the session, the husband was quite exasperated, and said, "But we have made up since. I knew my wife went to her work very angry that day, but since coming here I have learned that I should not withdraw so much from her, so I decided at the end of the day to go to pick her up from her work. So I did, and when I saw her I said to her, 'Are you still so angry with me?'"

The wife said in the session, "Of course when he asked me that, I just instantly melted inside. How could I stay angry when he asks me in this way? I just laughed and took his arm and I felt so happy and we walked home together."

When I asked the supervisee what did she think was happening for her during this session, she said, "I think I know now. My mum had such an angry way to attack my father. He was a little man, and my mum was a big woman. So I stood up for my dad and stood in front of him to protect him from my mum. This woman reminds me of my mum and this man reminds me of my dad."

In the next session with her clients, the supervisee did a beautiful job of bringing some of this insight into the session with the couple, and said something like, "I missed connecting with you about your anger." She invited the woman to say how it had been for her. The wife said she had felt very unheard and ill at ease after the session. And she said, "Now I feel so much better hearing what you have to say. Thank you for telling me this."

This supervisee had not shared with me in detail her feelings about her parents' dynamic, but we had briefly talked about her position in her family of origin before. Because the understanding was there from the beginning that these dynamics can get in the way, we were able to lightly touch on them and move on.

In another example, Robert (a pseudonym), a male supervisee, says he wishes to show me a piece of video in which he got angry with the male partner of a couple whom Robert describes as defiant. Robert had worked hard at clarifying the pattern the couple is getting caught up in. At the end of a session, the male partner asks "for some clearer instructions that I can work with at home." Robert describes feeling angry and as if all the hard work he had done up until that moment was disqualified by this man's request. Robert says he started to get defensive and went into explaining the work he was trying to do. Robert felt unhappy about this interaction and about getting angry and feeling devalued.

We talked about this, focusing on what feelings this partner's request had brought up – something about not being seen in the hard work and not getting recognition. It seemed it was just like at home with four older brothers and his father, where it was so hard for Robert to get recognition, and to get a sense of his self-worth with all that male competition and being the youngest. Robert said, "I cannot bear to be criticised, and this man's request felt like a criticism."

We role-played with Robert being the client, and then with Robert being the therapist.

After the role play, Robert said, "This man really wants to know how to get help with getting back on track with his wife. He cannot relate to some of the ways we were talking, he needs to be valued for wishing to take responsibility for getting the relationship to work better. I can see now that it was my own sense of having been dismissed by this man that got in the way."

After this supervision session, I realised I had not said anything about how courageous yet again Robert had been to show a piece in supervision in which he is dissatisfied with himself as a therapist. So I wrote him an email to say that, and also to say that just as he so much wanted to get credit for being more than good enough, so this male client probably was also yearning to get this validation.

To which Robert responded that, "Yes, I had felt quite vulnerable showing this, so thank you for saying this to me. I was wondering after the session, is it wise to bring such a piece, how will you see me as a therapist after that? But then I thought surely it will be good to use the session, especially when I am feeling exposed and vulnerable, so I can keep learning until the very end of my life. So my clients are helping me just as much as I am helping them . . . In this case, it is such a painful place when I feel criticised and it brings up this feeling in me. I am sure I have felt humiliated and belittled when I was young, and I missed feeling my dad was proud of me, that he saw my qualities, so part of me has such a negative self-view that I just cannot get it right. It is a deeply buried sense, and it does help to look at it . . . like a bird on the wire I try in my way to be free."

I then answered, "When you bring this to supervision, I see how courageous you are, and that yes, I see that right there Robert is experiencing feeling triggered by something and so does not have access to his great therapeutic empathy and skilfulness, so looking at this will be of benefit. I also think in bringing this, you will really be of such help to your client because you know how painful it is not to get recognition."

After the next session with this couple, Robert wrote, "This session was a big success. I told the man that I had watched the tape of the session, and that I was not at all proud of myself, that I had taken his request or comment too personally as a criticism of me. I had felt dismissed about the work with them I was trying to give my all to, and had gotten defensive instead of really hearing what you had to say, and that was really such a shame because you bravely had stuck out your neck and gave me some honest feedback how I could help you better and I could have stayed with that."

The man responded by saying, "No, it is my fault, I often get people to be defensive with me because of my way of talking to them."

Robert says he could see from the corner of his eyes the wife melt away, that she saw her husband say something about himself that was an opening also between them. At the end of the session, the man said, "I had wanted to stop the sessions, but now I would really like to continue."

How shall we draw this together?

Witnessing the ability of supervisees to reflect upon the way their therapeutic work is having an impact on them as human beings and is resonating on their personal stories has been very moving for me these last years. More than ever before in my professional life do I see this as a key point in helping the supervisee maintain a strong and working therapeutic alliance with their clients. It is my belief that the PPD work greatly enhances a supervisee's ability to reflect on their internal dialogue or experience. Having come to almost the end of my professional life (I am 68), I see PPD work, whether done individually or in a group format during the training, as a corner stone in the training of systemic therapists.

This brief process gives us a chance to deepen our empathy for our clients, having been encouraged to become more aware of, or explicit about, something that touched us. It also helps us deepen our understanding of what it is like to get caught up in the system or the negative cycle of the particular couple or family we are working with. It is as if we, as therapists, like the clients we are working with, are learning to make friends with parts of ourselves that we had pushed away out of fear or shame. By recognising the human beings we are, it seems that we can return to being fully available and emotionally present to our clients. After all, this is what all of us, as therapists, aspire to do.

I want to thank the supervisees who gave me permission to use the above examples of their process.

References

Casement, P. (1985) *On Learning from the Patient*, London: Routledge.

Flaskas, C. (1996) *The Therapeutic Relationship in Systemic Therapy*, London: Karnac.

Flaskas, C., Mason, B. and Perlesz, A. (2005) *The Space Between: Experience, Context and Process in the Therapeutic Relationship*, London: Karnac.

Hardy, V.K. and Lazloffy, T.A. (1995) 'The cultural genogram: key to training culturally competent therapists', *Journal of Marital and Family Therapy*, 21: 227–37.

Hildebrand, J. (1998) *Bridging the Gap: A Training Model in Personal and Professional Development*, London: Karnac.

Hildebrand, J. and Speed, B. (1995) 'The influence of the therapist's personal experience on their work with couples', in J. Van Lawick and M. Sanders (eds), *Family, Gender and Beyond* (pp. 331–8), Heemstede, The Netherlands: LS Books.

Johnson, S.M. (1996) *Creating Connection: The Practice of Emotionally Focused Couple Therapy*, New York: Brunner/Mazel.

Rober, P. (1999) 'The therapist's inner conversation in family therapy practice: some ideas about the self of the therapist, therapeutic impasse and the process of reflection', *Family Process*, 38(2): 209–28.

Satir, V. (1987) 'The therapist's story', in M. Baldwin (ed.), *The Use of Self in Therapy* (pp. 17–25), Binghamton, NY: Hayworth Press.

Yalom, I.D. (1995) *The Theory and Practice of Group Psychotherapy*, New York: Basic Books.

Chapter 7

Supervision and attachment narratives

Using an attachment narrative approach in clinical supervision

Arlene Vetere and Rudi Dallos

This chapter will offer an exposition of an attachment narrative framework in individual clinical supervision and for personal and professional development (Dallos and Vetere 2009). Central to this is the idea that the supervisory relationship is fundamental and, like the process of therapy, embodies the concept of a secure base from which the supervisee feels safe to explore their clinical practice. Much has been written about the secure base but it is important to note that how it develops is a fluid, dynamic and complex process that involves an integration of theory, personal reflection and relational empathy. Put simply, how this develops varies from person to person, and what may feel 'secure' for one person (e.g. moving to discuss sensitive feelings) may not feel safe for another, whereas focussing on concepts and theory may likewise feel distant and unsafe for someone else.

One way to think about this is that the supervision process is also informed by the idea of internal working models (IWMs), which constitute how the therapist and the supervisee see themselves, each other and their relationship. The IWMs develop from our early and subsequent attachment relationships with key people in our lives, and in turn guide and influence our relationships with our clinical clients. They feature our explicit and implicit assumptions about trust and safety in our relationships and about how we can manage our own emotions and feel safe enough to turn to others when necessary for support. These IWMs consist of multiple representations – embodied, sensory, semantic, narrative and reflective/integrative – and supervision needs to connect with all of these to help the supervisee integrate their representations of their client and the relationship with them at multiple levels. This means that supervision needs to be multilayered (e.g. in employing experiential activities, narrative development, visual representations, such as sculpting and role play, and with personal reflections).

A central feature of this approach is that attachment ideas are employed in a reflective way such that the supervisee is encouraged to reflect on how their own attachment experiences (e.g. in their own families) resonate with their experience of the clients/families with whom they are working. In turn, this process also applies to the supervisor in relation to their own experiences both inside and outside the supervision. This reflexive positioning for both supervisor and supervisee assists in focusing on their supervision relationship and importantly, in turn, with both their relationships with the clients, directly for the supervisee and indirectly for the supervisor. Thus, we see the significance of the systemic concept of triangular relationships: supervisor, supervisee and client(s) (Dallos and Vetere 2012).

Attachments and narratives

Imagine this training scenario. We are teaching on a supervision course. We open the session with the trainee supervisors by exploring the link between personal experience and professional practice. We use the following attachment narrative focused activity:

1   We invite the trainee supervisors to think of their first (or earliest) experience of being supervised.
2   We ask them to think of a word or phrase that captures the nature (or an aspect) of their relationship with that supervisor. We then ask them to think of a specific memory that exemplifies the experience.
3   In pairs, we direct them to discuss what they have learned from this experience and how it might have shaped and influenced their own developing supervision style.
4   We invite them to reflect on what they wish their current supervisees to learn from their experience and to take into the future of practice.

We have been surprised by what trainee supervisors have remembered in this activity. For example, some have described their earliest memory as feeling humiliated by their supervisor, and that they felt a need to apologise for their obvious mistakes and perhaps felt not good enough. Some have described that subsequently they decided they would try to avoid being that kind of a supervisor. On the other hand, one clinical psychologist described, with tears forming in his eyes, that Dr X "had him backed up against a wall and tore him off a strip." He went on to say he cried afterwards but now recognises that the experience "did him good and toughened him up!" This might sound extreme, but in fact we have been amazed at similar stories of supervision as a far from pleasant or secure experience.

So what is remembered from such early experiences? During the subsequent feedback session for the above activity, we often ask, "What came first – the memory or the word?" In doing this, we are introducing the idea of representational systems and the notion that our representations of our relationships are both complex and multilayered. Memory research suggests that we hold memories in interconnected networks: procedural memories of how we do things; sensory memories of emotion and sensation; semantic memories of ideas and beliefs; episodic memories of sequences of events; and integrative memories that draw on all representational memory resources (Tulving 1983; Crittenden and Landini

2011). Our internal working models, or dispositional representations, as Crittenden calls them, are that collection of beliefs and expectations about our own and others' behaviour that guide our actions, thoughts and feelings. The implications for supervisory practice are significant. The sensory and episodic memories are implicit, and powerful feelings may arise, of which we do not understand the origins or causes. For example, if the supervisee or supervisor, or both, feel threatened in a difficult moment, when one or both fears they will be seen as less competent, or failing in some respect, these representations may become activated. Fears about our acceptability to others may be raised, along with fears that others may not be available and concerned about us. Such fears are associated with high and unhelpful physiological arousal, and we become preoccupied in the moment with our own process. This can reduce our capacity for processing negatively laden material and our ability to read relationship cues. In our example above, the clinical psychologist was on the point of tears (somatic memories) as he described how the experience had been "good for him" (semantic representation). Importantly, despite being a competent and experienced clinician, he did not seem aware of the contradiction between these states. Our strategy for coping in these difficult and physiologically arousing moments might become activated, and could lean towards a deactivating strategy, or perhaps towards becoming emotionally overwhelmed as we struggle to manage ourselves and calm down. The naming of these early experiences and realisation of their continuing impact and of their potential for resonance and mirroring is an important first step in the processing and resolution of these memories.

In both psychotherapy and supervision broadly, we are promoting integrative and reflective thought processes, for all participants in the triangle of supervision. This is enabled by a sense of relative calm. A sense of calm is helped by soothing, compassion and listening. When we are unhelpfully aroused, say anxious or afraid of criticism, it is harder to be curious and reflective as we are more likely to be reactive and rely on 'old' solutions. In these difficult moments, we may over-rely on one representational system (e.g. semantic or procedural). If we are overly semantic, we may become rather abstract in our thinking and struggle to connect with a client's lived experience; or if we are overly procedural, we may become concerned with telling the client what they need to do, and so on. Thus, good listening is essential to promote a sense of feeling heard and of being deeply understood. These difficult moments challenge both participants in the supervisory relationship, and may well mirror client/supervisee interactions. Thus, the shared ability to work towards safety so that vulnerability and challenging experiences can be illuminated and talked about is at the heart of this approach.

In both therapeutic work and supervision, curiosity and creative problem-solving require trust and the ability to rely on the accessibility and responsiveness of the other. Reflective practice can be seen as a relationship between reflection and intuition in how we come to know what we know, and what we do not know. In systemic supervision practice, we emphasise the relationship between content and process in any conversational exchange, and the ability to comment on this process is supported by a sense of felt security in the relationship. Thus, the supervisor's job is to help the supervisee settle into the supervision relationship such that they can take emotional risks, expose potential areas of vulnerability, and realise strengths and interpersonal resources. In this way, the supervisor is also looking after the supervisee's relationships with their clients. Similarly, the supervisor also needs regular supervision of their supervision practice to identify potential obstacles to development of the supervision relationship and to promote a creative flow of ideas and experiences.

Thus, the supervisory relationship can be seen as the context for reflective learning and development. It provides a secure base for exploration and a safe haven when reassurance is needed; it provides a structure with clear roles and boundaries; it requires a commitment from both participants; the supervisor can be a role model, as can the supervisee in the context of reflexive education; and formative feedback can ground a developing sense of competence and confidence in an ever-emergent professional identity. In systemic thinking, we cannot wholly separate personal development from professional development as they are conceptualised as a dynamic equilibrium or tension of mutual influence from which professional identity is seen as an emergent property or higher context marker.

Supervision and the arousal of anxiety

Supervision is a relationship, it is a process, and it is a context for professional practice. In each of these domains, there is the potential for one or both participants to experience anxiety and unhelpful physiological arousal. Our work is subject to scrutiny and regular professional surveillance, in which we may identify and explore our errors of understanding, our mistakes and our prejudices. Although there are established differences in influence, roles and responsibilities in the supervision relationship, they are subject to negotiation, renegotiation and development, and both participants are subject to the normalising gaze of the other. There may be implied and unspoken or specific ideas of what constitutes good practice, and both are subject to the same social and professional practice discourses. Hence, the content/process distinction in a systemic process of supervision helps the participants negotiate how they will conduct their work together (i.e. 'talks about talks') and forms the platform on which they jointly critique the cultural ideas and practices that they draw on in order to make sense of complexity in relationships and in order to know how to go on.

When a supervisee is worried about their work, or worried about a client, we prompt an *attachment narrative focussed* discussion as a context for reflection and emotional processing. Following the description of the source of worry, we might explore how the therapist is creating a secure base and encouraging emotional risk-taking. We might use some or all of the following prompt questions:

1 For example, how is the client supported in developing a more integrated narrative of their experiences?

2   We explore how comfortable, secure or anxious the therapist might be feeling in the work with the client, and whether the therapist notices any defensive processes they might be using.

3   What attachment figures and relationships does the client arouse for the therapist and the therapist for the client?

4   How might the client's defensive processes be impacting, influencing and connecting with the therapist? What can be talked about? How? What feelings and thoughts might be defended or excluded?

5   What representational systems does the therapist prefer, and what is the fit with the client and with the supervisor? Is there an anxiety-blocking thought?

6   What, in the above discussion, is triggered for the supervisor, and thus for the supervision triangle?

Reflecting team conversations in supervision groups

The above questions can be modified for use in supervision groups with trusting and probably long-standing collegial relationships. More usually, we will adopt the following format to create a team reflection, either structured around some live therapeutic work or around a description in supervision. We would invite each group member to comment:

1   For example, what words or phrases in the description particularly struck them, and why? What did it evoke?

2   In the description, did they hear or experience the client/family as using any particular metaphors, and did any come to mind while they were listening to the description of the family?

3   What personal connections did the description or family conversation evoke for them?

4   Did the group members feel altered in any way as a result of listening to the description/family talking?

Systems ideas and power: variety and constraint

In any supervision discussion, we are interested to address the question of wider system constraints on what is possible, in the context of the therapy and what supports the therapy, and in the therapeutic and supervision relationships. In interpersonal systems, a wide variety of beliefs, explanations and stories are possible. Over time, and through a stochastic process of trial and error, some survive, endure and take on the status of a lived reality. In supervision, we acknowledge, explore and contest some of the constraints on variety. For example, we acknowledge our position in the system, such as our roles and responsibilities, which at times may overlap and not always be clearly defined. We explore the relationship between power and powerlessness and the inherent paradoxes of feeling powerless while being perceived as powerful. We differentiate personal and structural power, identifying where decision-making sometimes lies in other parts of an organisational hierarchy and our ability to influence those decisions, or hand them back, as appropriate. Inevitably, we acknowledge the limits of our power and influence (e.g. on local policy and practice), and supervision may provide the context for persistence in the face of disappointment.

Unchallenged and misunderstood emotional processes in relationships and teams, such as fear in the professional system, might interact with family and professional scripts and traditions of practice to constrain curiosity and therapeutic risk-taking. Similarly, intergenerational learning in family and organisational life cycles can intersect with developmental experiences of attachment, transition and change to either support or impede thinking and action in difficult circumstances, such as moral dilemmas in the therapeutic work. Any options to deconstruct dominant discourses and stories and to enhance awareness of other constructions or possible stories can be enlivened with a compassionate and gentle approach, and with proper time given over to these processes. And of course, this brings us back to the question of emotional safety in supervision and therapeutic relationships, and the respective responsibilities of all participants to develop and maintain the secure base for exploration, and to create the safe haven, for times of need, such as for reassurance and comforting.

The hallmark of good supervision is listening, and when supervisees feel anxious, a deep sense of feeling understood helps them to calm themselves and relax into the necessary work. A secure emotional connection in the supervision relationship promotes positive threat mediation. Our ability to learn and stay curious is based in a relationship of effective dependency where the supervisor is responsive and remains accessible (Gottman 2011; Johnson 2014). While we recognise that supervision is not therapy in the formal sense, it is therapeutic and provides a context for learning, resilience and empowerment that go beyond the boundaries of the supervision meetings into many aspects of the supervisee's life and that of the supervisor.

Some useful ideas for supervision from the narrative and systemic traditions of practice

The systemic and narrative traditions of therapeutic practice share some ideas and approaches that can be useful in the supervision process. Their isomorphism with therapists' practical experience can quickly foster thoughtful exploration of dilemmas and constructive problem-solving. The practice of relational reframing, exploring dominant discourses, such as pathologising discourses, mapping the influence of problems and externalising the problem, exploring unique outcomes, including hypothetical and imagined outcomes, reflective conversations, such as interviewing the internalised other, and exploring interpersonal versus essentialist explanations offer some helpful examples. This section will outline some exercises that draw on the above ideas and that further incorporate attachment-based thinking to explore the attachment significance of some therapeutic and supervisory encounters.

Interviewing the problem

This activity can be done in groups of two, three, four or five. Roles are allocated: a person with a 'problem'; a person role-playing the 'problem'; an interviewer; and an observer/reflector/supervisor. If only two people are present, some creativity is involved in changing roles of interviewer, observer and reflector! The exercise starts with an interview of the 'problem' while its 'owner' listens and observes, and then following the interview offers some reflections. Some prompt questions for the ensuing discussion could include the exploration of ways of: (a) how the 'problem' is asserting influence; and (b) how the influence can be blocked. (a) For example, asserting influence: What effect do you have on X's life and relationships? Describe, explain and give examples. What helps you to have this influence? Describe, explain and give examples. How does the 'problem' keep this influence? For example, divide and rule, cause conflicts, foster secrecy and so on. (b) Similarly, we can ask questions about how the influence of the 'problem' can be blocked. What makes it difficult to assert your influence on X's life (e.g. humour, being ignored)? Describe, explain and give examples. What was the time or moment when you first started to realise you were losing some of your influence on X's life? Describe, explain and give examples. Can you imagine what needs to happen for you to lose most or all of your influence? Who is best at reducing your influence? What actions are best at reducing your influence? What does it feel like when you realise you are losing your influence? What do you try to do to regain your influence? Who do you turn to? Who lets you back in (White and Epston 1990)? We find that this process of questioning leads to lively and constructive conversation that often leaves interviewees feeling liberated from the constraints and heavy burden of the 'problem', with a renewed and refreshed approach to how to go on.

Internalised other interviewing

This activity draws on the therapeutic application of internalised other interviewing to adapt it for supervision practice with individuals and groups (Tomm 1999). This is a useful activity when the therapist feels 'stuck' with the client, or struggles to hold empathy for the client. The therapist identifies their internal representation of their client, or their working model of their client, and tries to imagine how their client might feel, think and act. The supervisor conducts an interview with the therapist's internal other. The supervisor addresses them by the client's name, and explores their thoughts, feelings and actions as if they were the client. The supervisor might explore the following: How do you feel about working with your therapist? What is helpful, unhelpful? Does your therapist remind you of any attachment figures/family members in your life, past and present? What problems do you most/least want to focus on? How do you make sense of your problem? How do you think your relationships impact on the problem, and how do you think the problem impacts on your relationships, and so on?

Internalised other interviewing is a powerful activity in that it can evoke deeply held feelings. As a precursor to this activity, we often use a warm-up exercise, particularly if we are supervising a group or a team of therapists. Two people are invited to get into a pair where they know each other reasonably well. The supervisor then interviews person A as if they were person B for about five minutes. Person B listens during this time. Then the supervisor interviews person B as if they were person A for about five minutes while person A listens. Following this, all three discuss the two interviews: What did this feel like? How accurate were they? What surprised each of them about what the other said?

Exploring patterns of comforting

Giving, seeking and taking comfort is central to attachment theory. Our ability to self-soothe enables us to regulate our emotional arousal in difficult interactions. Our willingness to turn to others for help, support and comfort correlates with our experiences of felt security in our close relationships. Similarly, our willingness to accept comfort, without feeling inadequate or undeserving of care, correlates with high levels of self-reported well-being (Mikulincer and Goodman 2006). The following exercise can be done with a supervisor or a peer mentor as part of a personal exploration of our relationship to comfort, and thus how it might affect our responses and positioning in the therapeutic work. The systemic emphasis within this activity is on intergenerational learning and our ability to compare and contrast our experiences as we learn from them.

The activity opens with the following prompt: When you were upset or frightened as a child, what happened? The activity then continues with the following exploration: How did you get to feel better? Who helped you to feel better? How did they do this? What have you learnt from this for your own family? What do you want to do the same? What do you want to do differently? How do people comfort each other in your own family/relationships? How do you comfort your children? How do they comfort you? What do you want your children to learn from you about comforting? What implications does this hold for your practice? What cultural significance shows in how we offer, seek and receive comfort in our close relationships?

Conclusion

In concluding this chapter, we hope we have shown how we can use ideas from attachment theory and systemic theory in the *practice* of supervision and personal and professional development. We encourage you, the reader, to adapt and fit these activities and exercises to your own learning needs and working contexts. We trust they are sufficiently flexible that they can incorporate and integrate diverse ideas from the wide field of counselling and psychotherapy, and importantly that they help promote reflection and self-reflexivity in relation to all aspects of our work.

References

Crittenden, P. and Landini, A. (2011) *Assessing Adult Attachment: A Dynamic-Maturational Approach to Discourse Analysis*, New York: Norton.

Dallos, R. and Vetere, A. (2009) *Systemic Therapy and Attachment Narratives: Applications in a Range of Clinical Settings*, London: Routledge.

Dallos, R. and Vetere, A. (2012) 'Triangles and triangulation: a possible bridge between systemic theory and attachment theory', *Journal of Family Therapy*, 34: 117–37.

Gottman, J. (2011) *The Science of Trust: Emotional Attunement for Couples*, New York: Norton.

Johnson, S. (2014) *The Love Secret*, London: Piatkus.

Mikulincer, M. and Goodman, G. (2006) *Dynamics of Romantic Love: Attachment, Caregiving and Sex*, New York: Guilford.

Tomm, K. (1999) 'Co-constructing responsibility', in S. McNamee and K.J. Gergen, *Relational Responsibility: Resources for Sustainable Dialogue* (pp. 129–39), Thousand Oaks, CA: Sage.

Tulving, E. (1983) *Elements of Episodic Memory*, Oxford: Oxford University Press.

White, M. and Epston, D. (1990) *Narrative Means to Therapeutic Ends*, New York: Norton.

Chapter 8

Self and world

Narrating experience in the supervisor/supervisee relationship

Jim Sheehan

Introduction

The perspective unfolded in this chapter concerns the character and potential of dialogue in counselling and psychotherapy supervision as a process of transformative learning (Mezirow 1991) for both supervisors and supervisees. The chapter shares in the basic premise articulated by Stratton (Chapter 2, this volume), which views the many different forms of training and personal/professional development as contexts of adult learning. The supervisory event is one such form that belongs to the broad range of activities that constitute the personal/professional development of the practitioner, whether as part of their training or ongoing development. Several authors (Stoltenberg 2005; Creaner 2014) have understood the central function and purpose of supervision in counselling and psychotherapy as the development of capacities in supervisees, within a framework of regulated standards, that relate to their understanding of, and effective engagement with, the client contexts they meet on a daily basis within their practice. While affirming these critical supervisory functions, this present chapter finds its own unique perspective by drawing as much attention to the processes of supervisor learning and transformation as it does to those same processes in the supervisee. Hence, the reader can expect a very personal style of writing as I recount some episodes of my own learning and transformation as a supervisor alongside the transformative experiences reported to me by supervisees. A further premise of the chapter is that the development of relevant capacities leading to an extended performance repertoire within the domain of the supervisee's therapeutic practice is intimately bound up with the development of the selves of the supervision participants in parts of their lifeworld outside of counselling, psychotherapy and supervision. Hence, the purpose of this chapter is to throw more light on these other potential fruits of supervisory dialogue that often remain in the shadows as the supervision participants grapple with the realisation of supervision's central purposes. The reader should note that the perspectives unfolded here have much in common with those described by Jensen (Chapter 3, this volume), who asks about the influence of the personal life of the therapist on their therapeutic practice, as well as about the influence of the therapist's professional practice experience on their own lives.

As supervisors and supervisees narrate experiences and perspectives of different kinds to each other, they engage with a multiplicity of worlds to which they belong independently of each other, as well as with the world of supervision that they now share. What is mediated in these exchanges, I suggest, is a host of different *selves-in-worlds*. The chapter shares in the twin assumptions of Paul Ricoeur (1981, 1983, 1985), a French philosopher whose works in hermeneutical phenomenology spanned a 40-year period at the end of the twentieth century, that there is no self without a world in which that self can recognise and know itself, and that there is no world without a self to apprehend that world and respond to its features. 'Self' and 'world' are interdependent concepts that describe different aspects of personal experience and, consequently, must be thought together.

The general narrative character of both psychotherapy and supervision exchanges has been recognised for quite some time (White and Epston 1990; Schafer 1992; Sheehan 1995, 1999, 2004; McLeod 1997; Monk *et al.* 1997). The 'telling' by the client system of their personal and relational experiences takes on narrative-like form and structure as speakers attempt both to seek and give meaning in and to the lived experiences that form the content of their telling. In time, the supervisee's 'telling' within supervision of the focal client story as told by them in the context of the therapy also takes on a narrative-like form before the subsequent dialogue between the supervisor and supervisee builds further retellings of different kinds of both the focal client story, as well as of the context of its telling in therapy. All of these retellings take on a narrative-like form.

Now, if the character of these exchanges is like a *narrative* or story, the potential of the exchanges is *transformative* – transformative for the supervisee and transformative for the supervisor. And these exchanges and interactions have the capacity to be transformative because of the dwelling side by side within each of some aspects of either the client stories or the subsequent supervision narratives about those stories and other worlds of their own experience. The transformative learning potential, I will suggest, arises out of an intersection within each of the participants of some *world* emergent from their supervisory dialogue and some particular *world* of their own experience.

The chapter will explore two questions. First, *what* actually happens to the two participants in the supervision dialogue as they develop their exchanges and inquiry about a unique focal client story? And, second, *how* does this 'happening' occur? In the next section of this chapter, against the background of a particular supervision vignette, I will be summarizing some aspects of Ricoeur's narrative hermeneutics (the science and art of interpretation) and proposing that certain aspects of this hermeneutic framework offer resources which throw light upon both of these questions. In the subsequent section, I will describe three further supervision vignettes from my supervision practice with three different supervisees. In each vignette, I will be examining the transformative learning opportunities (Mezirow 1991; Mezirow *et al.* 2009) that seemed to arise for both supervisee and supervisor in addition to commenting upon the work involved in both 'outer' and 'inner' dialogue that seemed a necessary component of the progress within each along the pathway that stretches from their perception of transformative potential to its realization in their respective lifeworlds.

One additional comment is necessary prior to commencing. While it is expected in the *practice* of supervision that the supervisor would facilitate the supervisee in examining the connections between the focal client story, the therapy and their own worlds of experience, it is also assumed that any parallel examination of connections between the story told by the therapist of their experiences in the therapy (a story in which the case story is embedded) and the life experiences of the supervisor would remain, for the most part, an internal examination within the supervisor in the context of the supervision itself. However, in the *writing* about such supervision (of which the vignettes in this chapter are an example), that internal examination can find external expression and reflection (Burke 2006). Hence, I am going to put equal emphasis in the writing of these vignettes on my own opportunities for transformative learning as a supervisor. Such process will highlight the way in which *writing* about supervision can be a key tool in the self-supervision of the supervisor (McCormack 2010).

Ricoeur's narrative hermeneutics and the context of supervision

Vignette 1: Patricia and Jim: 'motherhood', 'fatherhood', 'parenthood'

Patricia is a 35-year-old social worker and family therapist. She is married with three children under the age of 6 years. She is employed as a counsellor/psycho-therapist in an adult mental health setting. At the time of the supervision described below, Patricia was in the final year of a four-year master's programme in Family and Systemic Therapy. The supervision was part of a module called Retrospective Supervision, which required her to undertake 50 hours of face-to-face supervision in which she reported and reflected upon therapeutic work from her practice setting. *Jim*, the author of this chapter and Patricia's supervisor, is a 65-year-old social worker, family therapist and systemic supervisor. He has been married for 25 years and does not have children. The vignette described here concerns the relationship of the participants to the themes of 'motherhood', 'fatherhood' and 'parenthood' in the context of both therapeutic practice and supervision practice.

In examining some of the DVDs of the supervision with Patricia during the time span of our work, I noticed how the early phase of our meetings was often occupied by a narrating on her part of some recent happenings in her own parenting experience with her three young children – perhaps a story of some minor child illness or some story of developmental growth. While I appeared to listen empathically to these stories, I recalled that my inner dialogue went something like this: "I think I need to allow Patricia a few minutes to report these experiences. Then perhaps we can get down to the real business of supervision as I am sure she has a few cases she needs to discuss and we only have an hour and 15 minutes left." When, on reviewing some of the DVDs of our work, I noticed this pattern in both 'our' outer dialogue and 'my' inner dialogue at the start of our meetings, I was somewhat shocked at my own blindness in not understanding this part of our dialogue as authentically an integral part of the supervision process and not simply some 'social' prelude to the 'real' supervision. I made a conscious decision to try to listen and engage with this 'preliminary' dialogue should it reoccur in whatever form.

The following session commenced with Patricia telling me how relatively good she felt as she had a full night's sleep the night before – her first in a long time. This had only happened because she had stayed overnight in Dublin (she lived 200 kilometres north of Dublin) alone, away from her husband and three children, in order to be on time for an early morning supervision meeting with me in advance of a full training day. I enquired about her more usual sleep patterns in the context of looking after her two young children as well as her recently arrived infant daughter (she was on maternity leave at the time). This led to a much more extensive dialogue about her coordination of feeds for her infant, an hour's sleep for herself here and there, being awake for her 'older' young child at 7 a.m. to 'breakfast' her and bring her to the playgroup, liaise and share some responsibilities with her husband who does shift work, as well as trying to stay psychologically in tune with the demands of managing the transitions in her children's sibling group as their numbers went from two to three. She took a pause in her narration, after which she uttered the following summarizing comment: "The whole thing is frigging crazy"– a comment spoken as a throw of her head slightly to one side was accompanied by a mildly hysterical laugh. I found myself listening very much more carefully on this occasion as I responded: "I know, I know." However, internally I asked myself if I really 'knew'. And if I 'knew', what kind of knowledge was this? Indeed, this 'knowledge' seemed to come from listening to many, many stories of parents, across more than 40 years of professional assistance, recounting the multiple challenges of 'performing' parenting and family life as parents with young children. But I did not personally know sleeplessness arising from the demands of feeding my own young infants, did not personally know the anxieties of managing feeds in the context of my infant suffering reflux, and have not known personally the challenges of coordinating a professional work life with the demands of being a parent to infant children. As Patricia had evolved her own narration and summarized her experience of sleeplessness, the only connections emergent within myself were the periods of sleeplessness arising from holding and being held by my wife in the middle of the night on so many occasions as we tried to console each other in the seemingly endless tearfulness and sadness arising from our own unwanted childlessness. It was an experience of sleeplessness that usually came to its own ending in an exhausted sleep that still allowed me to get up at the usual time and get on punctually with my working life. It was not a sleeplessness that required predictable periodic 'feeding' or its coordination with the management of response to the needs of a number of dependent, intimate others within the same household. In short, my experiences of sleeplessness seemed very, very different.

Patricia's pathway of 'outer' and 'inner' dialogue: Patricia continued narrating her experience of the challenges mentioned above for about a further 10 minutes before she seemed to arrive at a natural pause. After this shared natural pause in her narrating and my listening, I asked her the following question: "What do you think your experience of this stage of your life – with yourself, your partner, your children and your youngest being the age she is – will contribute to you as a therapist?" She replied in a further narration: "I think it is making me more understanding. It is arousing my curiosity more about how people actually manage. It makes me wonder how families survive on a day-to-day basis. It makes me really curious about the change when you add one (to the family). I mean, I think I am realising that chaos is a natural phenomenon. You do the thing you need to do to survive. I am actually giving her (her youngest child) a dummy now, a soother. You do anything to get a bit of sleep. My mother would have been very anti-soother. I took that over from her. But now I can see that in certain circumstances, your strong beliefs can go out the window . . . It also makes me think that just because you haven't gone through something doesn't mean you can't have a conversation with someone about it."

Jim's pathway of 'inner' dialogue: My earlier reflections that had taken me to a position of recognising how very different my experiences of sleeplessness were from those of Patricia slowly moved me to feelings of great sadness and some level of shock associated with recognising something for the first time. I began to face the fact that for many years, I had told myself that despite not having any children of my own I really understood very well the experiences of parents at any time of the family life cycle as a result of at least four decades of professional work with families. I began to see that this self-belief had led over many years to an impoverished kind of listening to parents about their experience due to the fact that somewhere inside myself, I felt I knew it all anyhow. A certain kind of sadness and sense of shame took hold of me for a period. The sadness now was no longer to do with being childless, but to do with a certain loss associated with many years of therapeutic work with families conducted without an adequate degree of reflection about the sameness and difference of my experience from that of many parents I had worked with. A sense of shame emerged that seemed clearly related to a feeling of being responsible for a certain degree of blindness related to a basic aspect of therapeutic practice. However, as I lived with this sadness and shame for a couple of weeks, these emotions seemed to give way to a new sense of humility, which found me listening much more patiently and carefully to the unique experiences of the unique parents who spoke with me in the context of my ongoing practice. The whole reflective pathway has allowed me to learn once more the art of being a student and learner in my own practice.

In this vignette, we can see how the supervisory dialogue and reflection on Patricia's experience of the demands of parenting young dependent children led to different kinds of reflective pathways for both supervisee and supervisor. But *what* exactly happened for Patricia and me within the context of this supervisory dialogue and *how* did it lead to the particular transformations that were realised for her in terms of an altered positioning within her therapeutic practice and for me in terms of new ways of positioning myself within both my supervisory practice and my therapeutic practice? I want to turn now to some aspects of Ricoeur's narrative hermeneutics to explore how they might throw light on these two related questions.

Ricoeur's narrative hermeneutics

At the heart of Ricoeur's narrative hermeneutics is the concept of *mimesis*, a concept that he borrowed from Aristotle's *Poetics* (1895) and subsequently developed in his own way. For Aristotle, the central activity at the heart of poetry and drama was 'the imitation of action' (*mimesis praxeos*) and what was produced therein was a plot (*muthos*) of some kind. In Ricoeur's (1983) development of the concept of mimesis, he subdivided the idea of 'the imitation of an action' as it applies to any type of narrative work into three different stages of *representation*, which he refers to as mimesis one, mimesis two and mimesis three. While it is the third stage of mimetic activity that is of most relevance to the two questions at the heart of this chapter, I will briefly describe here what is indicated for Ricoeur in the two earlier stages of mimesis.

The core idea at the heart of Ricoeur's three stages of mimesis is that of 'figure'. What is meant by this? When we tell ourselves or someone else about something, we provide ourselves or the other person with a figure of the thing we are telling about. What we have before us, then, is not to be understood as an exact copy of the thing spoken about, but a 'figure' through which the thing is represented. So, building on this core idea, Ricoeur identifies the first stage of mimesis with the concept of *prefiguration*. By this, he means that for both writers and readers of any narrative production, for narrators and listeners engaged around any story, human action already carries a meaning in advance of its portrayal within any particular spoken or written narrative. By virtue of their belonging to a shared culture the participants in the narrative production have a pre-understanding of the order of action – that is, they have a prior familiarity with the conceptual network relating to action. They 'know' the network of terms which include 'action', 'goals', 'motives', 'agents', 'accountability', 'circumstances', 'suffering', 'acting with others' and 'outcomes' of different kinds. It was thanks to this shared pre-understanding of the conceptual network relating to action that Patricia was able to narrate to me her experience of managing the care of her three young children and that I was able to follow her story about this part of her life and what it meant to her.

The second stage of mimetic activity for Ricoeur is signified by the term *configuration*. This is the activity at the heart of any narrative work that turns the telling of a range of different human actions, agents, events and circumstances into a meaningful whole. It is the representational activity that produces a plot through the process of turning a succession or sequence (this happened first, then that happened, and then something else occurred) into a *configuration*. In other words, the sequence of actions and circumstances narrated is configured as a story or plot of a particular kind. In this vignette, Patricia told a story about her motherhood of three young children and how the effort to coordinate a variety of simultaneous demands was, in a certain sense, "frigging crazy." My own listening to this story commenced in me an 'inner' dialogue and reflection which began to acknowledge the distance and difference between my own experiences and those of Patricia and issued in a story which questioned my sense of entitlement to believe that 40 years of professional work with families ensured my capacity to understand well enough the experiences of any parents and that my own childlessness had no bearing on the matter. In other words, I *configured* elements of my own experience in a new way.

It is Ricoeur's third stage of mimetic activity that is critical for the questions at the heart of this chapter. This third stage is signified for him in the term *refiguration*. Refiguration refers to the moment when the mimetic activity at the heart of any narrative work is joined to the life of the reader or listener (Ricoeur, 1985). For Ricoeur, the mimetic activity at the heart of any narrative or poetic work only reaches its full potential when "the work deploys a world that the reader appropriates" (Ricoeur 1983: 50). It is this idea of appropriation at the heart of refiguration that I will utilise here to give further underpinning to the idea of transformative learning for the supervisee and supervisor arising out of their supervisory dialogue. What a reader receives from the reading of a narrative text, says Ricoeur, is a world or worlds proposed by the text. The reader can make this world their own once they perceive it as a world that could potentially be inhabited by them. What the narrative or text offers is not some specific meaning placed in the text by the author or co-authors, but it offers, rather, "the projection of a world, the proposal of a mode of being-in-the-world which the text discloses in front of itself" (Ricoeur 1981: 192). In the language of Wittgenstein (1953), the text offers the reader 'new forms of life'. For Ricoeur, it is these new modes of being-in-the-world revealed by the narrative text that give the reading subject new capacities for understanding himself or herself. For myself and Patricia, we were the first 'readers' of the narratives produced in either our shared 'outer' dialogues or our respective 'inner' dialogues.

Returning to the vignette, we can see that Patricia's own reflective pathway, as well as our dialogue about her experience as a parent, produced a narrative in which she found herself being puzzled about the way she coped as a parent in her own life and what it meant for the sibling group in her family to move from two to three in number. However, the refigurative process commenced for her when an intersection took place between her personal *world* as a parent and her *world* as a therapist meeting with parents of young children. The narrative that produced a more puzzled and inquiring mother as she looked inward towards herself, her partner and their children proposed a 'figure' of selfhood that she was able to 'appropriate' into her world of therapeutic practice in the form of a more 'curious' disposition towards the coping mechanisms of young parents whose families were growing in size like her own.

With regard to my own transformative process, this emerged out of two different kinds of intersection. The first concerned an intersection between the *world* emergent from the narrative about Patricia's experiences of parenthood and my own *world* of childlessness. This intersection occurred initially, it would seem, out of a perceived resemblance on my part between these worlds around the theme of 'sleeplessness'. These worlds were similar in that sleeplessness was a feature of both but different in that the basis of sleeplessness was perceived as unremitting parental responsibility in Patricia's world and as arising from shared couple grief around childlessness in my own world. However, it was within my own subsequent 'inner' dialogue that new narratives emerged that offered me new possibilities in the context of other intersecting worlds. In particular, a narrative emerged that cast doubt on my long-held belief that, despite my own childlessness, I understood very well the experiences of parents at any stage of the family life cycle. The emergence of this 'narrative of doubt', as I might call it, led to other narratives that projected before them possible worlds in which new 'figures' of both supervisory and therapeutic selfhood were offered for appropriation. These figures of selfhood were marked by a careful, patient and more humble listening position, and were appropriated by me into both my supervisory lifeworld, where I listened to Patricia's (and other supervisees') experience in a new way, and my therapeutic lifeworld, where I found a new way of being with parents as they spoke of their parental experience. In the language of Ricoeur's mimetic terminology, my supervisory and therapeutic selfhoods were 'refigured' and renewed through the appropriation of new ways of being with parents that were part of the worlds projected and proposed by narratives issuing from both my inner dialogue and the 'outer' supervisory dialogue.

The mimetic passage from therapeutic dialogue to supervisory dialogue to lifeworld

Let me now describe the pathways of representation within the supervisory dialogue that lead towards the possibilities of refiguration for the selves of both supervisor and supervisee in their lifeworlds. I invite the reader to relate this description to the diagrammatical representation of this process in Figure 8.1. The first thing to recognise is that there would be no meaningful supervisory dialogue without some prior therapeutic dialogue. This fact is represented in the oblong box at the top of the diagram. What this box represents is the step of the client's narration of their problematic story to the therapist with whom they then have a dialogue in which are produced other narratives about the problematic story. The kinds of mimetic activity that are operational at this level are both *prefiguration* (both therapist and clients share in a pre-understanding of the order of human action and the conceptual network of terms associated with it) and *configuration* (the client narrations contain emergent plots and the subsequent therapeutic dialogue produces further plots with varying degrees of similarity to the plots emergent in the client narrations).

At stage two of the diagram, the second oblong box represents the moment when the therapist/supervisee meets the supervisor for a supervisory dialogue, which includes both the supervisee's narration of their therapeutic experience (with client story embedded) as well as subsequent dialogue with the supervisor in which new and other stories are produced that relate to the supervisee's experience in the therapy. At this stage, the kinds of mimetic activity that are operational in their dialogue parallel those at work in the therapeutic dialogue – in other words, both supervisor and supervisee share in a pre-understanding of the order of human action (*prefiguration*) as well as jointly producing a range of new and other stories (*configuration*) about the supervisee's therapeutic encounter from within the heart of their own supervisory dialogue.

However, there is a further moment within the supervisory dialogue when the third level of mimetic activity commences. Signified by the term *refiguration*, this moment is reflected in stage three of the diagram where the two square boxes side by side reflect the possibility of similar kinds of processes occurring in both supervisor and supervisee. These processes are initiated in each through the perception of resemblances of some kind between some aspects of the worlds projected by the web of narratives they have just jointly produced and some parts of their own lifeworlds. This perception of resemblance sets up within each a kind of intersection between worlds in which the worlds projected in their web of narratives offer themselves for appropriation by the selves of the supervisor and supervisee within their own lifeworlds.

The fourth stage of this mimetic passage is reflected in the two side-by-side square boxes at the base of the diagram and refers to the moment when the supervision participants (supervisor and supervisee) actually appropriate new forms of *self-understanding* through the performance of new ways of being, acting or feeling in certain parts of their own lifeworlds. It is at this level that we see the completion of the *refigurative* process commenced in stage three. When taken together, we can see that the refigurative processes operating at stages three and four of our diagram are the very stuff of the transformation potential attaching to supervisory dialogue. It needs to be emphasised, however, that there is nothing automatic about this kind of transformative process. It is not as though once an intersection between the projection of a possible world and some aspect of the supervision participants' lifeworlds has been set up through the perception of resemblances of some kind that change in the actual lifeworld is inevitable. More usually, the perception of resemblance is experienced as an invitation to a *labour of dialogue* (which can be internal, external or both), which may in time oversee the passage from the perception of new possibilities for the understanding of self in the lifeworld to the actual performance of new ways of acting, feeling or being in that same lifeworld. In each of the vignettes described in the next section, attention will be paid to elements along the pathway of dialogue's labour for each of the supervision participants as they move in the space between their perception and reception of new possibilities to the realisation/actualisation of these possibilities in aspects of their lifeworlds.

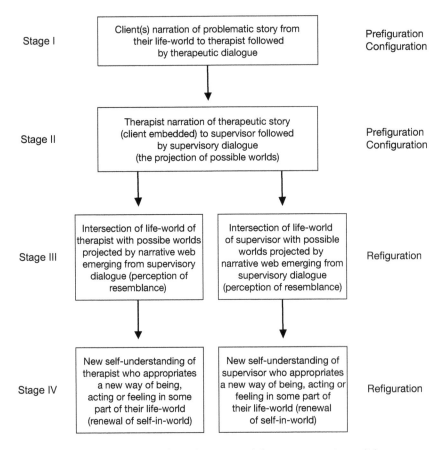

Figure 8.1 The mimetic passage from therapeutic dialogue to supervisory dialogue to lifeworld

The refigurative process in supervision

The following three supervision vignettes are offered here as further illustrations of the deployment of the above framework in the context of supervision practice. All the vignettes described refer to one-to-one, face-to-face supervision meetings between the author, who is a supervisor, and individual supervisees. In each vignette description, the emphasis will be on examining the processes in the supervisor, the supervisee and their supervisory dialogue that led to either the actual renewal of 'self-in-world' for both or the perception of opportunities for such renewal. Each vignette description, except for Vignette 2, will commence with a brief profile of the supervision participants (supervisor and supervisee) in addition to a note on the context of the supervisory relationships.

Vignette 2: Patricia and Jim: 'loss', 'anxiety' and 'protection'

Patricia and *Jim* are the same supervisory pair that featured in the vignette described in the last section. The vignette presented here is concerned with the themes of loss, anxiety and protection.

One of the 'cases' brought for supervision by Patricia in her final year of training was that of a 35-year-old single male called Donald. Donald came to Patricia's service for therapeutic support due to a mild depression following the death by suicide of one of his six closest friends, a 32-year-old single man called Frank. Donald had been significantly impacted by the death of his friend, who he knew to be struggling over questions linked to his sexuality. Frank had been the eldest of four siblings whose parents lived apart. He had confided in Donald his despair over what he anticipated would be the inability of either of his parents to accept him should it turn out that he was either gay or bisexual. Frank had died through self-poisoning from a balloon filled with helium gas, which he had taken back to his apartment following his younger sister's birthday in his mother's home. Donald was distraught about whether he could have done more to protect his friend in his emotional crisis. These were the basic elements of the therapeutic story narrated by Patricia to me.

While the supervisory dialogue considered many aspects of both the case story itself and the therapeutic relationship, I had the feeling within our dialogue that we were still on the edge of something that might be more relevant for Patricia in the context of the case. I asked her the following question: "From all that we have discussed so far about Donald, Frank and his family, and your relationship with Donald, is there any aspect of the whole context that you would like us to dwell upon a little further?" She immediately replied in a more engaged manner that the thing she found most challenging in the case was the helium balloon. What was it about the helium balloon that she found challenging? It was that something that seemed superficially so harmless and usually connected to fun could be the vehicle through which the life of this young man was lost. It made her feel hopeless in some way that was not yet clear to her. We had an initial dialogue about her feelings of hopelessness and the only observation she could make at the time was that such feelings might be connected in some way to her own three young children. We ended our conversation about the case at that point and did not return to our dialogue for another month. However, it was clear that a reflective process had been initiated both between us and in both of us about the helium balloon. During that interim period, part of Patricia's module task was to write up brief notes on both the therapeutic session discussed as well as a self-reflective note following her supervisory dialogue with me about the case. The following paragraphs will recount the reflective train that was set in motion within each of us.

Patricia's pathway of 'inner' and 'outer' dialogue: When we came back to our dialogue about the case two months later, Patricia told me that the relatively short discussion we had previously about her emergent feelings relating to the case had made her think about aspects of her life with her three young children. It made her feel hopeless and helpless at first at the realisation that she was not going to be able to protect her children from every possible danger they might encounter – no matter how hard she would try. She had recently had the experience of allowing her 5½-year-old daughter to commence attending a dance class on a Saturday afternoon. The case, our dialogue about aspects of her own experience, as well as her own ongoing inner reflection had made her realise that she could never protect herself from the anxiety about the possibility of prematurely losing one of her children. The train of her reflection had made her think more about how she would actually cope and what she would do if such a calamity were to happen. Surprisingly, she had found that this whole reflection had helped her to manage better the anxiety about such a potential loss. She had noticed that she was able to drive her daughter to the dance class, bring her safely into the class and then go off and attend to some of her own personal business for the next hour before collecting her daughter after the class. Prior to this reflective process, she had anticipated that she would be waiting outside the class in her car and keeping a watchful, scanning and anxious eye on the immediate surroundings of the dance class for any possible danger from which she might have to protect her daughter.

Patricia's anticipated image of herself as an anxious, babysitting, waiting-outside-the-door kind of mother was replaced by a different kind of maternal feeling that gave her more choices concerning the performance of her own parenthood. In the terminology of Ricoeur's mimetic framework described earlier, the configurative work at the heart of both the case and the supervisory dialogue led to a perception of resemblance within Patricia between the world of her client, wherein tragic loss had occurred through the medium of a balloon, and the world of her own parenthood, wherein she endeavoured to protect her young children from all danger. This perception of resemblance marked the commence-ment of a refigurative process in which an amount of internal and external reflective labour produced narratives that projected possible worlds in which parental anxiety associated with the possible tragic loss of a child was managed in a relatively contained way. In Patricia's context, she clearly appropriated these newly projected possible modes of being-in-the-world as a parent and the refigurative process was completed in her through the performance of a new kind of parental feeling and behaviour in certain parts of her lifeworld based upon a new form of self-understanding.

Jim's pathway of 'inner' and 'outer' dialogue: Following the dialogue about the case, including the symbolism that the helium balloon had gathered through Patricia's initial expression of hopelessness connected in some unclear way to her young children, I found myself initially struck by the vulnerability of Patricia in relation to her young children, as well as by the enormous loss for Franks's parents and siblings arising from the tragic death of their son and brother. While the therapeutic story, in addition to my two dialogues with Patricia about her experi-ence in the therapeutic relationship, evoked many different stories and scenarios in my own life, the experience to which my attention was most drawn was a very current scene in my relationship with my partner.

For the previous year or two, I had become quite gripped by an anxiety relating to the possibility of losing her through death. A variety of different fears had taken hold of me. I had become very worried about the possibility that she would have an accident in the car as she made a weekly long journey to visit her ageing mother. I had become very worried about the possibility of her being attacked while out walking alone. I had been worried about her having an accident while cycling to work in the early morning during the summer months. I had been worried about her being attacked and killed in our home while I was travelling away for work. My anxiety had driven me to be quite controlling in different ways – advising her about where and when not to walk alone, advising her about the distance she must keep her car from the car in front of her on wet roads, advising her not to forget to put on the alarm and double-lock the doors when I was away in addition to a host of other 'reminders' and 'advice'. The case study and my discussion with Patricia led me to think more about the way my anxieties were pushing me towards certain kinds of controlling behaviours in my relationship with her that were becoming overbearing, annoying for her and somewhat destructive for us. As my inner reflection developed, I found myself facing more directly the anxiety about the possible loss of my partner from my life, as well as the limits to the protection I could provide over the possible loss of myself from her life through accident, illness or sudden death. I began to think about the practical ways I might cope on a day-to-day basis should I lose her from my life. As time went on, I could see that this whole reflective labour seemed to have the effect of diminishing greatly my personal anxieties regarding such potential loss and generated in me a more carefree disposition towards the risks associated with both of our lives and the 'time' of our relationship. At the same time, I noticed that my range of overbearing protective 'reminders' in our shared daily discourse seemed to go into hiding.

In the terminology of Ricoeur's mimetic framework, a refigurative process seemed to commence in me when I perceived a resemblance between Patricia's world of parenthood, wherein her anxiety about possible harm to her children kept her in an ongoing position of hyper-vigilance, and my own couple world, wherein anxiety about the potential loss of my partner led me to maintain an unrelenting protective discourse within the context of our daily life. The subsequent supervisory dialogue with Patricia about her own reflective pathway and stories about transformation in her own life projected a possible world in which a subject contained their anxiety about the potential loss of a loved one. This figure of anxiety containment was appropriated by me and the refigurative process was completed, following the pathway of reflective labour noted above, in the performance of an altered couple discourse, which allowed my partner to get on with 'the dance class' of her own life without carrying the burden of my anxieties.

Vignette 3: Therese and Jim: 'illness', 'protection', 'letting in' and 'letting out'

Therese is a teacher and family therapist in her middle eighties. She has been a member of a female religious community in the Roman Catholic tradition since she was 18 years of age. She worked as a school principal for many years before she retired as a teacher. She trained and qualified as a family therapist in her mid-fifties before going on to develop her own private practice in family therapy and individual counselling. She commenced supervision with me in my private practice when she was 57 years of age and has now been in supervision with me for just over 25 years. I was 40 years of age when I commenced meeting with Therese for supervision. I am now 65 years. Therese is part of a group of eight siblings, one of whom is now deceased.

Two months prior to the drafting of this chapter, Therese brought the following case to supervision. She told me that a very attractive 31-year-old woman, Tara, had commenced therapy with her. She was the youngest of five siblings and the only one to remain living with their parents in the family home. While two of her older siblings had experienced problems of different kinds over several years, she had done well at school and had succeeded in obtaining and keeping an administrative job in a small local voluntary hospital. She had had some health problems and was taking some medication for gastritis, a hiatus hernia and some oesophageal symptoms. However, she had these medical issues under control and she explained that she was coming for therapy because she experienced her life as very constrained. She did not have a boyfriend and she simply did her work and returned home every evening. While she tried to engage in social activities in the community, she found that her efforts in this regard led to no particular enjoyment for her.

Therese told me that as Tara was trying to clarify for herself during the second and most recent session what she wanted from being in therapy she (Therese) found herself drawing on her pad a sketch of someone dressed in a suit of armour. She decided to turn the pad around to show it to Tara, who immediately said: "That's like me!" As Tara looked at the pad and Therese encouraged her to say more about what she saw, Tara made the further comment: "There's a bitch in there and I am not sure if I want to let her out." As our supervisory dialogue unfolded, Therese clarified that the matter she wanted to reflect upon most with me concerned her own positioning as a therapist with Tara. She expressed her concern in a specific question: "Should I be pushing her a bit more?" Our own supervisory dialogue then evolved around this question, with Therese commenting upon how awful a waste it would be if this talented young woman was to be unable to realise her potential as a human being (a thought that made her want to 'push' Tara a bit down the path of coming out a bit more from behind the suit of armour) and myself responding with a question that wondered whether the therapy needed a push at this moment, given that it seemed that her own intuitive response within the therapy (allowing herself to make the sketch that she showed to Tara) seemed to initiate an unfolding reflection within the client that appeared already to be gathering its own momentum. As we reached a pause in this part of our dialogue, which I thought had reached a kind of conclusion for that day, Therese said in an excited voice: "Oh – you are really making me think today . . . you have really got me thinking!" I asked her what she meant. She replied: "I was just thinking about a new teacher we had in school when I was 11 years old. She said to me one day in the class, 'Therese, I can't teach the class while you are like that.' You see, I had complete control over the class of my peers. Complete control of them and of myself. But I had a protective shield on." She paused for a moment or two, with the excited expression appearing to give way to something more challenged as she commented: "Oh, you are getting me to dig deep today! I think I am still a bit like that – with the shield." With this comment, the supervision concluded for that day.

Therese's pathway of 'inner' and 'outer' dialogue: When Therese returned one month later, she came to talk about Tara as the third case she wanted to speak about that day. She commented that Tara had really started to 'fly' and had begun to try out doing different things for herself. She went on to say that she realised she was quite like Tara in many ways herself. She had felt that she too was enclosed within something. She had begun to realise that she did not easily let things in to reach her. She had found herself thinking about this as she was doing some of her regular spiritual reading. She went on to speak about the work of one author for whom she has a special regard. This particular religious/spiritual writer, she noted, continually emphasises how much we are all loved by God. Therese commented that while she really liked this idea, she knew she never really let this idea reach very far inside her. However, now she had found herself beginning to both accept and to feel that she is really loved – not just by God, but by people around her who she meets every day.

For Therese, a refigurative process was commenced with her perception of a resemblance between her client Tara's world in which she seemed personally encased in 'a suit of armour' and her own past childhood world of being a pupil in school and her current world of spiritual reading as an adult in religious life. The web of narratives emerging from her own reflection, as well as from the supervisory dialogue about her work with Tara, projected a world in which a subject laid down their protective shield and let things from the outside world reach them a little more. This refigurative process was completed in her as she appropriated the elements of a less protected self projected from the supervisory dialogue and appeared to experience herself as more receptive in the context of both her spiritual reading and the world of her daily meetings with those around her.

Jim's pathway of 'inner' and 'outer' dialogue: Between the first and second of these meetings with Therese, I found myself feeling very connected to this young female client of Therese through her medical symptoms. Therese had reported three of Tara's medical symptoms, which were the very same complex of symptoms and conditions that had emerged for me during a recent period of illness and medical investigations. I was also struck by that part of our supervisory dialogue in which Therese had noted that she still had a protective shield. These themes about illness, control and protective shields that either kept things from getting out or getting in had set me thinking as well. It set me thinking about how I used my work life as a shield. My working day rarely ended by 6 p.m., and more usually continued for a further few hours in the evening, not to mind finding its way into different parts of the weekend. I rarely took breaks during the day as one work-related task flowed seamlessly into another. The need to keep my work under control led me to keep pushing myself to meet self-imposed punishing deadlines. In the process, I kept pushing down the voice inside me that was asking for more relaxation and, in particular, for some space to enjoy some fiction reading, which has always filled me with a sense of relaxation and a feeling of well-being whenever I allowed myself do it. I even approached my recent period of illness as something like a piece of work that I had to do something about and something I needed to control so that I could keep the rest of my work under control!

While it would be impossible in this short space to adequately account for the extent and range of reflections set in motion by the recognition of resemblance between certain themes emergent in both the therapeutic and supervisory dialogues and my own lifeworld, suffice it to say here that this reflective effort has moved me to a place where I am listening and responding more to that voice within me that wants more breaks during the day, wants to finish work by 6 p.m., and wants more chance just to have a quiet read. My thinking about my work pattern has changed from thinking about it as an addiction (which was often accompanied by a kind of reassuring inner comment that I could have worse addictions!) to a more focussed reflection generated by the conjunction of the themes of illness, control, protection and responsibility. A more permeable boundary around my work life and experience has fostered an inner world in which the voices representing the demands of work and the desire for relaxation hear each other a little better.

Vignette 4: Aoife and Jim: 'death', 'loss' and 'missed opportunity'

Aoife is a 53-year-old psychiatrist and psychotherapist who has worked solely in private practice in Ireland for the last 15 years, having had a prior career in the National Health Service in the United Kingdom. She is married and lives with her husband and their only child, a 12-year-old girl. She has been coming to me for supervision for the last eight years. She has a mixed practice, which includes psychotherapy with single adults and adolescents, as well as therapeutic work with families after separation and divorce.

Very recently, I got a text from Aoife, who normally comes for supervision on a monthly basis, requesting that we bring forward by one week our appointment for supervision, as there was some urgency about a case she needed to discuss. In the eight years I have been supervising Aoife, I have only had one other similar request from her. I found the space within a few days and we met. She described how there was a particular case that was keeping her awake at night over the previous two weeks. She was concerned about a possible bias emerging in her approach within a very complex case. The heart of the case seemed to revolve around divergent adult perceptions of the needs of a 10-year-old girl whose mother had died three years previously. The child's mother had been engaged in several years of conflict with her father about access following their separation when the child was 3 years old. She had not been married to her daughter's father, and just prior to her early death at 35 years of age she had made a request to all the adults involved in her daughter's life to allow her grandmother to play a central role in her daughter's future care. Because they were keen to avoid a potentially harmful and expensive legal conflict about the young girl's care, all the adults in the situation agreed to seek Aoife's assistance and advice in the matter.

When I asked Aoife what her concern was about her possible bias in the case, she told me, as her eyes began to fill up, that she was concerned about the power of the dying mother's wishes within her own thinking about the case. I invited her to try to say some more about her worry and she immediately told me: "It is something about this child being left . . . It is something so like Georgia (her own 12-year-old daughter) but not quite the same . . . Georgia is 12 now and just about to go into secondary school . . . she is leaving me through growing up . . . she just doesn't need me in the same way . . . this other child lost her mother . . . yet I have spent so much of my time running away from Georgia." Her tears had begun to flow more freely. Our ensuing dialogue moved back and forth between reflecting on the case and its challenges and Aoife's own past and future with her adolescent daughter. I asked her two questions about herself in relation to Georgia during this dialogue. The first concerned the past: "How would you like it to have been different for you with Georgia in the past?" To which she replied: "I would have liked just to dwell more in my love for her instead of running away from her and going to so many film festivals and other events." Shortly after this response, I asked her the following question about the future: "What would you want for yourself with Georgia in the future?" She replied: "I want to be able to delight in her development."

Aoife's preliminary pathway of 'inner' and 'outer' dialogue: It appeared that prior to our 'emergency' meeting, Aoife had vaguely connected her sleeplessness around the case to an anxiety about possible bias on her part in relation to her own thinking about the case process. However, in the very early part of our dialogue, she appeared to see a resemblance between the mother-daughter relationship at the heart of the case (where the relationship was foreclosed by death) and her own relationship as mother with her own daughter (where the relationship up to now seems to have been intermittently truncated by her own 'running away' from her daughter). Remember that she had noted at the commencement of her 'filling up' that "it is something so like Georgia . . . but not quite the same." This perception of a level of resemblance allowed her to access a reservoir of painful emotion that seemed to operate as the motor for further reflection within the dialogue. The configurative work at the heart of the case, as well as within our own supervisory dialogue, had projected possible worlds of parenthood that were joined to Aoife's own lifeworld of parenthood, thus commencing a refigurative process within her. The dialogue had projected in front of it a mode of parenting an adolescent daughter in which a parent 'delighted' in the young person's development in contrast to an experience of ongoing 'sadness' associated with the natural sense of loss associated with this phase of a young person's life. It remains to be seen how the particular reflective pathway opened up by the perception of resemblance noted above will lead Aoife to narrate and live the future of her relationship with her daughter or whether the energy around this reflective pathway will suffer its own kind of truncation.

Jim's preliminary pathway of 'inner' and 'outer' dialogue: The dialogue with Aoife about the case seemed to pour fuel into a number of different dialogues about myself in different worlds to which I belong based upon a number of perceived resemblances. In listening to the dialogue we created about Aoife, the case characters and their situation, I began to reflect upon: (a) the world of my own professional case practice and possible biases that might operate therein; and (b) my world of conversations with my partner about other parents and children that we know. However, the part of my own world that emerged as having the strongest resemblance with the worlds proposed by my dialogue with Aoife was the world of shared time and activities with my own partner.

I began to think about the possibility of facing in to my partner's death or mine with the feeling of having missed so many opportunities to spend time together because of the level of work I choose to undertake. The anticipated sense of regret was difficult to face and to bear as my reflection went forward. As Aoife might have said about the resemblance between the parent-child relationship in the case and that at the heart of her own life, it is 'the same' with myself and my partner but also 'a bit different'. The themes of death, loss and missed opportunity were the anchors upon which a relation of resemblance arose within me between the world explored in the dialogue with Aoife, in which the case story was embedded, and the world in which I enjoy the opportunities to spend time with my partner or avoid those opportunities under the pretext of work. This is the stage of this preliminary reflection, and it remains to be seen what the fate of this pathway will be. The perception of resemblance between aspects of both Aoife's case story and life story and my own world of missed opportunities with my partner commenced a *refigurative* process that has the potential to reach completion not just in a new understanding of self, but a new performance of selfhood in the couple part of my lifeworld.

Exercise: The double genogram

Leaving behind the stories of my own supervision experiences for a moment, I would now like to invite you, the reader, to explore a practice experience of your own through the following exercise. I have called this exercise 'the double genogram' because it involves placing side by side on paper two diagrams, each depicting a set of three generational relationships and the themes that were central to these relationships. On the left-hand side of the page, you should draw the diagram of the family relationships (grandparents, parents and children) in which your clients' lives are embedded, and on the right-hand side of the page you should draw a similar diagram relating to your own life. Now add in at the bottom of the pictorial representation of relationships on both sides a list of the key themes (e.g. 'parental separation', 'living away from homeland', 'loss of a parent in childhood') that seemed to be central to these relationships over time. Then stand back from your page for a while and ask yourself if there are any connections emerging for you between aspects of your clients' lives and relationships and aspects of your own life and experience. Write a few notes for yourself on another page about the most compelling connections that emerge for you and allow yourself to follow in your inner dialogue the direction that seems to be suggested by your observations about possible connections. Leave your pages aside for a few days before returning to them and adding any further reflections you may have had in the interim. Finally, ask yourself the following questions about which you can reflect at leisure: (1) If you had the possibility of learning something important for your own life as a result of a deepening reflection upon the connections between this unique piece of professional practice and your own unique life, what do you think it might be? (2) If you had the possibility of learning something important for this unique piece of professional practice from a deepening reflection upon the connections between your own life and the life context of the client(s), what do you think it might be? Briefly, then, the steps in the exercise are as follows:

- Step 1: Draw the two genograms (client and therapist) side by side on a single page, adding at the bottom of each side of the page the key themes.
- Step 2: Stand back from the page and consider possible connections you may be observing between the genograms.
- Step 3: Write some notes for yourself on another page about the most compelling connections that seem to be emerging and allow your inner dialogue and reflective process to follow the direction suggested by the observed connections.
- Step 4: Leave your pages aside for a few days before returning to add any further reflections you may have had in the interim and ask yourself the two questions (articulated in the previous paragraph) about important learnings for your own life and for this unique piece of practice arising from your consideration of connections.
- Step 5: Keep your notes at hand over the following days and add some notes recording your reflections on the two questions.

Readers should adapt this exercise in ways that are suitable for the piece of professional practice upon which they wish to reflect.

Conclusion

This chapter has explored the potential for transformative learning for supervisees and supervisors arising from their shared dialogues about clients that are the very meat of supervision practice in counselling and psychotherapy. Whether you are reading this chapter as a supervisor, counselling practitioner or student in psychotherapy training – or, perhaps, with a foot in more than one of these positions – you have been invited to consider some ways in which the web of different narratives you generate through dialogue with your 'other(s)' in supervision can offer you possibilities for new ways of being and acting not just in the context of the specific pieces of professional practice that have been the subject of supervision 'talk', but in parts of your own lifeworld that may seem far removed from your practice experiences. I have used a complex of concepts from the narrative hermeneutics of Paul Ricoeur to throw some light on the puzzling questions concerning what exactly happens in the supervision talks and how processes embodied in these talks seem to function for both supervisor and supervisee. It is my hope that you, the readers of this text, have been sufficiently engaged by some aspects of the theory, supervision vignettes and accompanying exercises in this chapter to enable you to explore your supervision experiences from some new angles.

References

Aristotle (1895) *Poetics*, introduction, text, translation and commentary by S.W. Butcher, *Aristotles' Theory of Poetry*, London: Palgrave Macmillan.

Burke, A. (2006) 'Do the write thing', in E.W. Taylor (ed.), *Teaching for Change* (pp. 79–90). New Directions for Adult and Continuing Education, no. 109, San Francisco, CA: Jossey-Bass.

Creaner, M. (2014) *Getting the Best out of Supervision in Counselling and Psychotherapy: A Guide for the Supervisee*, London: Sage.

McCormack, D. (2010) 'The transformative power of journaling: reflective practice as self-supervision', in M. Benefiel and G. Holton (eds), *The Soul of Supervision: Integrating Practice and Theory* (pp. 25-37), New York: Morehouse.

McLeod, J. (1997) *Narrative and Psychotherapy*, London: Sage.

Mezirow, J. (1991) *Transformative Dimensions of Adult Learning*, San Francisco, CA: Jossey-Bass.

Mezirow, J. and Taylor, E. (2009). *Transformative Learning in Practice: Insights from Community, Workplace and Higher Education*, San Francisco, CA: Jossey-Bass.

Monk, G., Winslade, J., Crocket, K. and Epston, D. (1997) *Narrative Therapy in Practice: The Archaeology of Hope*, San Francisco, CA: Jossey-Bass.

Ricoeur, P. (1981) *Hermeneutics and the Human Sciences: Essays on Language, Action and Interpretation*, edited, translated and introduced by J.B. Thompson, Cambridge: Cambridge University Press.

Ricoeur, P. (1983) *Time and Narrative, Vol. 1*, Chicago, IL: University of Chicago Press.

Ricoeur, P. (1985) *Time and Narrative, Vol. 3*, Chicago, IL: University of Chicago Press.

Schafer, R. (1992) *Retelling a Life: Narrative and Dialogue in Psychoanalysis*, New York: Basic Books.

Sheehan, J. (1995) 'Psychotherapy as narrative: a critical application of Paul Ricoeur's philosophy of narrative to psychotherapy', unpublished PhD dissertation, University College Dublin, Ireland.

Sheehan, J. (1999) 'Liberating narrational styles in systemic practice', *Journal of Systemic Therapies*, 18(3): 51–68.

Sheehan, J. (2004) 'Positioning narrative in psychotherapy', *Eisteach Journal of Counselling and Psychotherapy*, 3(3): 6–11.

Stoltenberg, C.D. (2005) 'Enhancing professional competence through developmental approaches to supervision', *American Psychologist*, 60(8): 857–64.

White, M. and Epston, D. (1990) *Narrative Means to Therapeutic Ends*, New York: Norton.

Wittgenstein, L. (1953) *Philosophical Investigations*, Oxford: Blackwell.

Chapter 9

Conclusion

Consolidation, celebration and momentum

Peter Stratton, Arlene Vetere, Helga Hanks,
Anne Hedvig Helmer Vedeler, Per Jensen,
Kyriaki Protopsalti-Polychroni and Jim Sheehan

> Transformative learning involves experiencing a deep, structural shift in basic premises of thought, feelings, and actions. It is a shift of consciousness that dramatically and permanently alters our way of being in the world . . . Transformative learning has an individual and a collective dimension, and includes both individual and social transformation.
>
> (O'Sullivan 1999)

What is at the heart of each chapter?

Personal and professional development is learning. It is the kind of learning that changes us, changes others and changes our relationships. Seeing adult learning through a systemic lens makes us think in terms of interactional processes of reflecting, monitoring and articulating (see Peter Stratton and Helga Hanks, Chapter 2, this volume). In this book, we have focused on PPD as the development of our repertoire of selves that we can use in our therapeutic and professional interactions to the betterment of everyone. In our framework, all the disciplines and all the psychotherapies have a shared core of developing 'the self of the therapist', albeit with different methodologies. Our hope is that the particular contribution of systemic integration as it has evolved over time enriches every approach.

We recognise the mutual and powerful influences between the different worlds we inhabit with their significant relationships – at home, at work, at play. Who and what we are and what we do at home influences who and what we are and what we do at work; and what we do and what we are at work influences who we are and what we do at home, for example. Our passion is to try to create a language that links personal processes and our professional practices (see Per Jensen, Chapter 3, this volume).

In this way, we are helped to stay alert to all these potential connections and to look after ourselves and each other (see Helga Hanks and Arlene Vetere, Chapter 5, this volume). Helping people take care of themselves is what enables us to work at the extremes of human experience, and to recognise the emotional impact of our work in its everyday manifestations. Supervisors help trainees to be aware in ways that do not challenge their emerging sense of competence and confidence in their ability to work, and for both trainees and qualified colleagues, to help them incorporate learning from these experiences in ways that enhance compassionate appreciation of our shared humanity.

As the reader, you will see how we have emphasised emotion, and emotional connection with attachment at its heart (see Arlene Vetere and Rudi Dallos, Chapter 7, this volume). We have tried to show how we can use attachment theory within a systemic framework to develop and use emotional processes in supervision for the benefit of the supervisee and their clients. Furthermore, in our ordinary supervision dialogues, we show how our one-to-one exchanges carry potential for transformation for supervisors as well as for supervisees (see Jim Sheehan, Chapter 8, this volume, and Anne Hedvig Helmer Vedeler, Chapter 4, this volume). We have included an account of a supervisor's personal transformative progression from working with PPD in training groups to working with experienced therapists in supervision that leads to an enhanced focus on emotions and emotional safety (see Barbara Kohnstamm and Arlene Vetere, Chapter 6, this volume).

We invite the reader into the challenge of how it is possible to create an isomorphic transformation of the training context and the trainees' development. We have regularly invited our readers to see PPD as a process that changes the supervisor just as much as it changes the supervisee. This facilitates the development of contexts where different roles and hierarchies are experienced at the same time and put together in a learning process.

Reprising the themes that connect

We have intended that our book will add new dimensions to PPD provision that create a shift towards a substantial upgrading of practice. We have theorised the shift and shown how it can be implemented across a range of professional contexts. In our opening chapter, we described five themes that underpin the approaches that each chapter has taken to its area. Here, we return to these as coordinating themes to help you consolidate the different ways you may want to incorporate them into your practice. It will also serve as a set of reminders about where in the book you can revisit these themes.

1. Self of the practitioner: developing the personal and the professional therapist, trainer and supervisor as systemically interlocking selves in interpersonal contexts

Systemic approaches to PPD have developed a variety of ways that enhance the practice of supervisors, supervisees, trainers and trainees. All the chapters emphasise the self of the practitioner across multiple roles and contexts. We propose that the usual function of personal therapy in training is replaced in systemic approaches by live supervision of practice that strongly emphasises the self of the therapist.

In Chapter 7, Arlene Vetere and Rudi Dallos introduce the idea of representational memory systems from attachment theory research to help us explore the layers of attachment and their associated meanings in our various roles. Supervision practice that relies on words and talk might inadvertently reinforce a semantic approach to experience that could exclude some significant sensory and emotional experiences in our various encounters as trainers, trainees, supervisors and practitioners. Arlene Vetere and Rudi Dallos advocate an active and reflective approach to support the integration of experience across all our memory systems, so that we might draw on all our shared resources when trying to promote well-being in our communities.

In Chapter 2, Peter Stratton and Helga Hanks liberate the idea of the self from an idea that it is a core stable definition of the person. It is more usefully talked of as an activity in relation to others. As the chapter moves to considerations of PPD as learning, they move to ways in which the self is defined through the understandings that the person acquires. This suggests considering PPD as a process of creating new selves – of the trainee, the supervisee, the trainer and the supervisor. The fact that these new selves are constructed in the interactional processes of these many roles has led them to the insights provided by theories of the dialogical construction of multiple selves. Thus, the progressive consideration of the selves of the therapist opens up ways of recognising the scope for PPD to use a variety of forms of interactional learning to give the therapist increased options in their practice.

In Chapter 5, Helga Hanks and Arlene Vetere discuss the strong connections and feelings experienced by supervisor and supervisee when working on specific cases containing child abuse and violent material. They consider how the stories of our clients can produce in both the supervisee and supervisor feelings of compassion that could lead to compassion fatigue or worse. They pay attention to the emotional safety of the trainee and the qualified professional in their practice.

2. Systemically caring for ourselves and our families: linking personal private life and professional practice

The importance of taking care of ourselves is an underlying assumption throughout each chapter in the book. In Chapter 5, it is more specifically addressed in terms of working at the extremes of experience, but we do not want this focus to take away from a necessary recognition of the impact of our different roles and our work on all of us, as seen in Chapter 4. At an extreme, the failure of organisations to care for staff can result in compassion fatigue, and even burnout. In this book, we have tried to emphasise the relational aspects of these phenomena and the shared and different responsibilities to address them, rather than seeing them as a failure of the practitioner.

A truly systemic position recognises the relationships between work, home and other significant contexts, and thus directly addresses what we bring home from work, and what we take to work from what is happening at home. For example, difficulties with sleeping and waking at night with palpitations, resonances with past bereavements and divorce, parallel connections when therapists and clients are in similar situations, and carrying inspiration and positive emotions from therapy to home interactions.

In Chapter 3, Per Jensen is looking for, and exploring, the patterns that connect narratives from therapists' personal and private lives with narratives from family therapy practice, and vice versa. This chapter is about the patterns that connect therapists' personal and private lives to their clinical practice, and their professional practice to personal and private life. Per Jensen presents 'the map of relational resonance' to show how therapists' private and personal narratives of their experience might influence their clinical practice. The other way around, this chapter shows how working as a therapist might influence personal and private life. That means that we are looking at what therapists learn from their clients and bring home – into their own personal and private lives.

Helga Hanks and Arlene Vetere, in Chapter 5, specifically address the importance of caring for supervisee, supervisor, family and individual clients, as well as the organisation we work in, partly constituted by these roles and people. They think about the material that we all have to listen to and sometimes experience – material that often reaches the edge of human behaviour, emotions and endurance. They discuss the consequences for those involved in such cases and how ensuing stress can lead to stress symptoms, compassion fatigue, secondary trauma and even burnout. Unmanageable stress is known to reduce the quality of work, the quality of personal relationships and the mental health of the worker. They discuss how our private lives are affected and how we need to take care of ourselves, and the systemic connections between the organisations we work in and how they function. Regular PPD activity and space for reflection can play a large part in helping workers look after themselves and each other in ways that predict and prevent burnout.

3. Narrative, and engaging with novelty through storytelling with attention to a positive working context: the central role of internal and external dialogue and the use of metaphors of PPD as journey

Storytelling through personal and poignant examples is found in each chapter. These are finely judged. Each author is committed to using these examples to describe, to explain, to illuminate, to process and re-process experience. Reflection and reflexivity emerges and is encouraged in this way. Thus, storytelling is used both as a technique in PPD activities across all our roles, and as a central process of our development – see especially Arlene Vetere and Rudi Dallos, Chapter 7, this volume.

Drawing upon some aspects of narrative hermeneutics, Chapter 8 demonstrated how the different narratives generated in the supervisory exchanges project 'worlds' of different kinds that offer themselves for 'appropriation' to the supervision participants in particular ways. The examples in the chapter show how what Jim Sheehan calls 'reflective/dialogical pathways' are set up within and between participants once either perceives a resemblance of some kind between one of the 'worlds' projected in the exchange and some scene in their own lifeworld. The participants then have the opportunity to perform and experience a 'refigured' selfhood in that part of their lifeworld, courtesy of the 'figure' of selfhood proposed in the projected world.

Throughout Chapter 2, the reader is invited into dialogue with their self and (preferably) with colleagues as routes to experiencing and integrating their learning and its implications for their practice. The stories that we tell ourselves are seen to be constitutive of the self of the therapist, but dialogues with supervisors and trainees emerge as powerful ways to introduce new possibilities in practice. The trick of PPD that will produce superlative practice is to create the conditions from which the most generative dialogues will emerge.

4. Reflection and reflexivity: and as it is also applied to the writers in the process of this book!

In a wider sense, reflection and reflexivity are common to the practice and theory of all disciplines and psychotherapies. We aim to create a working context that enables people to be calm and thoughtful about what is happening to them and others, to integrate experience across all their representational memory systems, in ways that promote cooperative practice. We see this thoughtful and quiet process enabled as it slowly unfolds in the telling of the supervision experience in Chapter 4.

In Chapter 6, Barbara Kohnstamm and Arlene Vetere explore the transformative journey for a supervisor across professional practice in two European countries and through the enhanced incorporation of an emotion focus in the work. Drawing on the work of Susan Johnson (2002), Barbara Kohnstamm outlines how the practice of emotional safety in supervision was realised through the explicit recognition of emotional resonances and their connection to our earlier emotionally significant learning experiences with our attachment figures. In this way, Barbara Kohnstamm shows how experienced practitioners have been helped to explore relational resonance in a way that enables them to take emotional risks in the supervision such that their practice with the client is supported – an emotionally grounded way of knowing 'how to go on'.

The approach to developing the self of the practitioner progressively spelled out in Chapter 2 drew first from the work of Kolb (1983) and Schön (1990) on experiential learning and educating the reflective practitioner. As the model developed, it placed central importance on the role of reflection on the therapist's learning processes. These processes are described in the spiral model (Stratton 2005). Reflection on the processes themselves gives the learner the reflexive tools for evermore efficient learning – which can then be applied to how they will learn from their practice. We saw these processes in action as we worked on the book:

pausing to reflect on our processes, so that we became sensitised to the needs of our potential readers but at the same time reflexively able to proceed in new directions and with new integrations.

Reflections and reflexivity take a central place in Chapters 4 and 5. Anne Hedvig Vedeler and Helga Hanks and Arlene Vetere discuss the loneliness of people reflecting in isolation. In some organisations reflection is often used as an assessment tool, and Helga Hanks and Arlene Vetere question whether this is the most creative way of being reflexive, particularly in supervision. All three authors propose that being reflexive in groups, sharing thoughts and listening to different viewpoints are effective ways to enhance our competence.

5. PPD as (adult) learning and the role of understanding learning in enhancing PPD

A basic position in the book has been to see all aspects of PPD as forms of learning. The learning reciprocally involves trainees and trainers, supervisees and supervisors. In fact, in our thinking, counselling and psychotherapy must also be a learning context for clients if useful change is to have lasting value. We have therefore throughout our work on the book tried to optimise the text as a series of learning opportunities for our readers. At the same time, we have been alert to the areas of practice that will be most useful for those pursuing PPD to learn more about while being guided by current understanding of how adult learning is optimised.

Chapter 2 is entirely devoted to approaches to learning that could underpin PPD. It provides a framework for integrating material from educational research into adult learning and organisational studies. While learning is known to be most effective when it is pursued as a dialogical process, there is also much valuable material in which it has been studied as an active autonomous process of the adult learner. While the authors of this book engage with systems thinking in their therapy practice, training and supervision, we know that major advances have been made in the wider applications of systemic sciences, and these too are briefly considered.

The theme of transformative learning found articulation in Chapter 8. Here, Jim Sheehan placed special emphasis on the opportunities for transformative learning for the supervisor arising from supervisory dialogue – opportunities that run alongside those on offer to the supervisee. Jim Sheehan emphasised the 'work' character of the interactional processes that are the ground of transformative learning.

What we have learned from writing this book

The close cooperative activity needed to write this book has helped us get to know each other even better! The shared commitment to showing how systemic thinking and practice can enhance all counselling and psychotherapy PPD activities has led to cooperation, the tolerance of ambiguity and of each other, compromise, humour, forgiveness and support for challenging positions. We have accelerated our engagement with our own development both on an individual level and within our many peer groups. We have taken risks in exposing ourselves and in writing down what we think and do. We have been irreverent to our deeply held assumptions about ourselves and others. This comes from our systemic paradigm. We recognise all of this has become part of us in all parts of our lives.

One of the things we struggled with in writing this book is the use of the term PPD – 'personal and professional development'. The term is used widely in professional circles in the UK, Ireland, Norway and the US. It is not always used in other European countries, and the political ramifications of the term need acknowledgement. For us, the term represents a unifying position of the personal and the professional, and highlights the difficulties in talking of one without acknowledging the other, almost as if they exist independently. In addition, the term 'use of self' causes discomfort for two of us because it seems to imply an objectification of the person – it is not an inclusive term. We also struggled with the individualistic and mechanistic assumptions within the concept of a person 'burning out'. We prefer multiple descriptions that capture felt experience, relational experience and organisational contexts because 'burnout' does not occur in a vacuum.

What is unique about this book?

In this book, we recognise the multiplicity of our roles as we train and develop as practitioners. We address the perspectives of the trainer and the trainee and the supervisor and the supervisee, during training and in lifelong post-qualification practice. Our systemic approach unifies the personal and the professional in PPD. It honours reflection and reflexivity as emergent properties of the process of integrative learning in PPD. We emphasise the co-evolution of our learning within our multiple roles, for ourselves and with each other. This is co-constructed through interaction, through dialogue, through developing trust by sharing experience, through re-storying our own experiences, through argumentation and sometimes through heated discussion!

Engaging our readers in active learning processes

Learning is central to PPD. In this book, we have exemplified our systemic philosophy of learning by trying to engage the reader actively through concrete examples and exercises. We have bravely confronted our assumption that PPD can become a comfortable routine that does not challenge and inspire development. The whole purpose of this book is to encourage readers to add new dimensions to their engagement with their own and others' development. We believe this leads to a substantial upgrading of our practice – knowing how to go on.

References

Johnson, S. (2002) *Emotionally Focused Couple Therapy with Trauma Survivors*, New York: Guilford.

Kolb, D. (1983) *Experiential Learning: Experience as the Source of Learning and Development*, Englewood Cliffs, NJ: Prentice Hall.

O'Sullivan, E. (1999) *Transformative Learning: Educational Vision for the 21st Century*, Toronto, Canada: University of Toronto Press.

Schön, D. (1990) *Educating the Reflective Practitioner: Towards a New Design for Teaching and Learning*, San Francisco, CA: Jossey-Bass.

Stratton, P. (2005) 'A model to co-ordinate understanding of active autonomous learning', *Journal of Family Therapy*, 27: 217–36.

Index

abuse: child 65–82; consequences of 71–2
accountability 44, 46, 78
action research, supervised therapy as 22–3
Ahola, T. 10
Andersen, T. 54–5
answerability 54
anxiety 70, 76, 79, 82, 86, 101–4, 120–1
appropriation 115–17, 120–1, 123
Aristotle 114
attachment 132–3; histories 87
attachment narrative 99–107; exercises/activities 104–6
attachment theory 106, 132–3
attribution 10

Bakhtin, M. 52
Bateson, G. 9, 13
being-in-the-world 115, 120
Bentovim, A. 70
Berg, I.K. 22
Blackmore, C. 26
blaming 82
bodily feeling 54–8, 60
Boland, C. 77, 78
boundaries 79
Bradbury, H. 23, 80
burnout 70–4, 133–4, 137; compassion fatigue 73–4; described 74–5; prevention 72; within systems 70–1, 77, 78; see also stress

caring for the practitioner 133
Carnevale, P.J. 27

Cecchin, G. 15
circular processes: between therapist and client 33–48; personal and private experience of 33–48
cognitive dissonance/reciprocal dissonance 41
compassion 65–6; compassion fatigue 73–4, 76, 133–4; see also burnout
configuration 114–16, 118, 120, 125
continuing professional development (CPD) 77–8
coping skills of therapist and clients 37–8
courage 36–7
courage expressed within therapy 36–7
creativity 26–7, 29; and research training 27; in systemic practice 13–15
Crittenden, P. 69, 101
Csikszentmihalyi, M. 6
curiosity 51, 62, 101, 104, 113, 115
cynicism as sign of burnout 74

Dallos, R. 99–107, 133
de Bernart, R. 89
De Jong, P. 22
Deslauriers, L. 17
deutero-learning see learning
diagnosis 11–12; treatment model in mental health 10
dialogue 18–19, 52, 112–13, 116–17, 119–20, 122–6, 132, 135; dialogical selves 25–6, 28; inner dialogue 25,

90–6, 110–13, 115–16, 119–20, 127;
  outer dialogue 110, 112–13, 115–16,
  119–20, 123, 125–6; supervisory
  dialogue 109–10, 113, 115–25;
  therapeutic dialogue 116–18
dissonance, reciprocal 41
Draper, R. 72

Elkaïm, M. 34, 38
emotion 132, 134; adult 136; emotional
  safety 133, 135; transformative 131,
  136
emotion-focused couple therapy (EFT)
  85, 90
emotional safety in supervision 86–7,
  104
empathy 41, 73–4, 82, 96, 105, 111
Epstein, E. 10, 23, 27
Ericsson, K.A. 9
evidence base 11
exploratory practice (EP) 22–3

fatherhood 111
fatigue 71–2
feedback 72, 81, 86, 88–9, 95, 100,
  102
Figley, C. 73–4
figure 114–16, 121
Firth-Cozens, J. 78
Foucault, M. 34
Friis, P. 53
Furman, B. 10

Gale, J.E. 11
genogram 3–5, 89; double genogram
  126–7; family and professional
  67–8
Gibbs, G. 17
Goolishian, H. 23
Greenhalgh, T. 11
grounded theory research 38
group facilitating 86–8

Habermas, J. 41
Hanks, H. 1–30, 65–83, 131–7
Hatcher, S. 35–7, 45
Hayward, M. 72
Hermans, H.J.M. 25–6

hermeneutics 110, 114–16, 134;
  hermeneutic cycle 8, 18
Hobbs, C. 70
Hopkins, J. 70–1

improvisation 53–4
internal working models (IWMs) 99,
  101
Ireland 85–8, 124, 137
Ison, R. 26

Jennings, L. 38
Jensen, P. 1–6, 33–49, 89, 109, 131–7
Johnson, S. 135

Kahneman, D. 15, 77
Kapuscinski, R. 51
knowledge, declarative vs. procedural
  8
Kogan, M. 11
Kohnstamm, B. 75, 85–96, 135
Kolb, D. 17, 135

Lamson, A. 73, 76
Larsen, H. 53
learning 131, 133, 135–7; adult 7,
  16–17, 22, 131, 136; approaches to
  increasing effectiveness in 11–13;
  deutero-learning 9; from clients 33–5;
  from relationships 36; higher levels
  of achievement and the self 7–11;
  learning spirals 18–21, 29–30, 135;
  reflective learning 9; reflexive and
  autonomous learning 16–22;
  transformative 131, 136
legal system, influence of 66
Leiter, M. 76
Lerøy, A.M. 35, 37
life story work 92
listening 112–13, 115–16, 124, 126

McGoldrick, M. 3
Magnuson, S. 3
Malloch, S. 53
management 76–7, 104, 133
Maslach, C. 76
Maturana, H.R. 26
Menzies Lyth, I. 76

metaphor: position of 8; using
    metaphors in practice 14–15
mimesis 114–18, 120–1; mimesis one
    114; mimesis praxeos 114; mimesis
    three 114; mimesis two 114; mimetic
    activity 114–17; mimetic framework
    120–1
model of influence in abusive systems
    70–1
modernism 62
Morgan, G. 14
Morrison, T. 72
motherhood 111
Munton, A. 10
muthos 114

narrating experience 109–28
narrative 23, 35, 45, 47, 55–6, 89, 100,
    104, 134; attachment narrative
    99–107; narrative hermeneutics 110,
    114–16, 134
National Health Service (NHS) 65, 67,
    124
Netherlands 85, 90–1
Norway 137

Olkowska, A. 44
Orlinsky, D. 45
overwork and consequences 71–3

parenthood 111
Parsons, T. 41
Payne, R.L. 78
perception of resemblance 117–18, 120,
    125, 126
personal life 134
personal and professional development
    (PPD): challenges 85–7; emotional
    and relational risk-taking 87;
    facilitation 85–9, 92; formative
    feedback 88; as a process of learning
    46–7; and resonance in practice 45;
    self-evaluation 88; use of
    photographs and images 89
personal therapy, effects on therapists
    45–6
phenomenology 110
playfulness 26–7

plot 114–16
Polychroni, K. 1–6, 131–7
power: power relations 34, 41–4;
    recognition of influence in therapy
    34–6; therapeutic imperialism and
    43–4
Practitioner Research Network 28
pre-understanding 114, 116–17
prefiguration 114, 116–18

reciprocal dissonance 40
refiguration 116, 119, 122, 124;
    refigurative process 115, 117–18,
    120–1, 123, 125–6
reflection 5, 24, 61, 79–80, 107, 133–6;
    reflective practice 23; reflective
    process 119–20, 127; reflective
    supervision 73, 99–100
reflexivity 5, 79–82, 134–6; self-
    reflexivity 81, 107
relationships 131; relational resonance
    135
representation 116, 127; stages of 114
resonance 134, 135; challenging
    reciprocal 40–1; with the
    environment 34; from practice to
    personal life 35–6; map of relational
    34–5, 38–9, 45, 46; personal
    resonance 34–5; reciprocal 39–40;
    relational resonance 34–5, 38–9; as
    seen within systems 34; therapeutic
    colonisation in 41–2; understanding
    resonance 34; within relationships 36
Ricoeur, P. 110, 114–16, 120–1, 128
Rober, P. 25
Rogers, M. 34
Rønnestad. M.H. 45
Rorty, R. 27

Saugstad, P. 41
schemas 27
Schön, D.A. 9, 17, 23, 135
SCORE 28
second loop learning 9
secure base, the 15, 27–8, 39, 88, 99,
    102, 104
self 133; assessment of 79–80; caring
    for 79–80, 131; creating different

24–6; dialogical construction of 25–6, 28; higher levels of learning 7–11; integrating personal and professional aspects 92; learning as part of developing 7–11; protection of 72; self-in-world 118; self-understanding 117–18, 120; selves-in-worlds 110; of the therapist/practitioner 90–6, 131–3, 135
self-supervision 111
shame 56, 59, 87–8, 96, 113
Sheehan, J. 1–6, 33, 46, 109–28, 131–7
Simon, G.M. 24, 28
Skovholt, T.M. 38
Smith, C. 22, 26
soft systems methodology (SSM) 22–3
Steiner, S. 22
Stern, D. 53
storytelling 134; *see also* narrative
Stratton, P. 1–30, 77, 109, 131–7
stress 66–7, 72, 74; helping supervisees to control 15; impact in workplace on 66, 70–1, 77–8
Sullivan, M.F. 38
supervision 67–8, 71–2, 75–6, 78; and the arousal of anxiety 102–3; and attachment narratives 99–107; coping strategies 101; cycle of poor 72; development of trust 99, 101; early experiences 100–1; emotional safety 104; internal working models (IWMs) 99; main responsibilities around 78–83; and narrative and systemic traditions of practice 104–6; and reflecting team conversations in groups 103; reflection on own attachment experiences 99; reflective 72; reflexive positioning 99; and the secure base 99, 102, 104; supervisor learning 109; supervisor progression 85–96; supervisory selfhood 116; systemic triangles 100–1, 103; systems ideas and power 103–4
supervision activities/exercises; exploring patterns of comforting 106;

internalised other interviewing 105–6; interviewing the problem 105
Sweet, J. 80
systemic approach 2, 12, 25, 88, 132, 137
systemic therapy 7, 22, 26–8, 85, 90, 96
systemic thinking 1, 12, 23, 102, 136
systems 65–83; burnout within 72; dysfunctional 77; ecosystems 68–9; family 65–83; management and 66; models of 70; and organisations 76–7; trauma organised 70
systems constraints 103–4

Tajino, A. 22–3
therapeutic colonisation: direct form of 43; as a family therapists culture 41–2; indirect form of 42–3; a special form of resonance 41
therapeutic imperialism 43–4; and power 44
therapeutic relationships 33, 38–41, 104, 119–20
Thomas, R. 74
trafficking children 70
training and PPD 12–13, 23–5
transformation 23, 52, 116
transformative learning 109–11, 115, 128, 131, 136
trauma 65–83; focused therapeutic work 78; secondary 73–4
Trevarthen, C. 53

Vedeler, A.H. 51–62, 131–7
Vetere, A. 1–6, 65–83, 85–96, 99–107, 131–7
violence 65–83, 133

well-being 66, 79, 124
Wilson, J.P. 74
Wittgenstein, L. 53, 56
work context 131, 133–4
world 110, 115–17, 120–1, 123, 125–6

Yalom, I.D. 88

Lightning Source UK Ltd.
Milton Keynes UK
UKHW022000080419
340709UK00008B/76/P

9 780415 730853